"If you are looking for a practical guide to help you or your church to understand how to evangelize within the natural rhythms of life, then you will find no better guide than *Witness* by Jonathan Dodson. Rather than giving us a set plan or method of ⟨…⟩ gelism, Dodson gently he⟨…⟩ pelling beauty of the gos⟨…⟩ s."

⟨…⟩ sions, ⟨…⟩ chool

"Jonathan Dodson's ⟨…⟩ ource that the church re⟨…⟩ athan thoughtfully tackle⟨…⟩ ⟨…⟩ceptions and unhelpful approaches to sharing Christ, as well as giving clear gospel insight and real-life wisdom, making it easier to sensitively speak of your faith. As part of the Love Your Church series, this book feels like a friend by your side, encouraging you to share Jesus with humble confidence. Perfect for anyone wanting to grow as a witness for Christ—whether just starting out or feeling weary and looking for fresh encouragement."

DAN STEEL, Principal, Yarnton Manor, Oxford

"Some books on evangelism feel like watching a professional BMX bike rider at the X-Games. We're inspired—awed even—but rarely do we think we could ever imitate what we're seeing. For many of us, stepping out of our comfort zone to share the gospel with others often feels more like a child learning to ride with the training wheels off. *Witness* is the kind of book that lands on you like the hand of a patient father on your back, guiding you forward despite all the wobbles, spills, and self-disappointment—into an encouraging rhythm that every believer can enjoy. Every chapter is biblical and beautiful! Jonathan has written a refreshing, practical, and gospel-saturated book that I can confidently put into the hands of every believer in my church to deepen their own confidence for living faithfully on God's mission."

ADAM RAMSEY, Lead Pastor, Liberti Church, Gold Coast, Australia; Director for Acts 29 Asia Pacific; Author, *Honor* and *Truth on Fire*

"What I most appreciate about Jonathan Dodson's instruction on evangelism is his attentiveness to the person who needs Jesus: a posture of kindness and care that shines through the clarity and compassion in his conversations about the saving grace of God. This book will equip and encourage you to listen in love and speak the truth of Jesus."

TREVIN WAX, VP of Resources and Marketing, North American Mission Board; Author, *The Thrill of Orthodoxy* and *Gospel-Centered Teaching*

"Warning: this warm, practical book will invite and encourage you to practice evangelism with joy, as it did for me. Whether you're scared to talk to others about Jesus, enthusiastic, or somewhere in between, *Witness* will equip you and your community to take real-life steps in sharing the good news."

RACHEL GILSON, Leadership Team, Theological Development and Culture, Cru

"As the body of Christ, we have been called to share the reason for our hope and our certainty in him. *Witness* is a must-read, then, for all of us who call ourselves disciples of Jesus. Through the pages of this short but powerful book, Jonathan Dodson urges each of us as individuals to think both practically and prayerfully through what it means to be faithful witnesses for Christ in our everyday lives."

VANCE PITMAN, President, Send Network

"In *Witness*, Pastor Jonathan Dodson skillfully guides readers into a holistic understanding of the church's missional work, anchoring our witness in the beauty of the gospel and the posture and practices that emerge from being captivated by Christ. Don't be fooled by its size—this small book is rich in insight and tangible application. It is a gift to the church."

REV. CLAUDE ATCHO, Pastor, Church of the Resurrection, Charlottesville, VA; Author, *Reading Black Books*

"*Witness* is a gem of biblical equipping, insightful illustrations, and practical examples for evangelism. Dodson can encourage you and your church to continue in the tradition of the early church."

J.A. MEDDERS, Director of Theology and Content, Send Network; Co-author, *The Soul-Winning Church*

witness

JONATHAN K. DODSON

thegoodbook
COMPANY

thegoodbook COMPANY   **ACTS 29**

Witness
Loving Your Church by Sharing the Gospel
© 2025 Jonathan K. Dodson

Published by:
The Good Book Company

thegoodbook.com | thegoodbook.co.uk
thegoodbook.com.au | thegoodbook.co.nz

Unless otherwise indicated, Scripture quotations are from The Holy Bible, English Standard Version (ESV), copyright © 2001 by Crossway, a publishing ministry of Good News Publishers. Used by permission. All rights reserved. All emphases are the author's own.

All rights reserved. Except as may be permitted by the Copyright Act, no part of this publication may be reproduced in any form or by any means without prior permission from the publisher.

Jonathan Dodson has asserted his right under the Copyright, Designs and Patents Act 1988 to be identified as author of this work.

Original series cover design by Faceout Studio | Art direction and design by André Parker

ISBN: 9781802543162 | JOB-008264 | Printed in India

To City Life Church (2007-2022):
though temporal, eternal.

CONTENTS

Foreword — 9
1 True Witness — 13
2 Faithful Presence — 27
3 Implausible Evangelism — 43
4 Biblical Evangelism — 59
5 Gospel Metaphors — 71
6 Community Evangelism — 85
7 Shameless Prayer — 95
Conclusion — 105
Acknowledgments — 109
Discussion Guide for Small Groups — 111

FOREWORD

BY ED STETZER

Once upon a time—maybe about a generation ago—many churches intent on making disciples lacked the resources they needed to equip their people for the task. In response to that need, denominations and parachurch ministries responded with a profusion of programs, tools, and methods to help churches and individual believers share Christ and grow disciples. Today we no longer lack resources. We are blessed with multitudes of them, from plans of salvation and presentations of the gospel to strategies for planting churches and tools for teaching the Bible.

But many churches still aren't thriving, especially in evangelism. We have the tools; what we need is people—people who are ablaze for God, on a mission to show and share the good news we have received. People who are filled with the Spirit and changed by the gospel. People who are burdened to pray and ready to proclaim the good news.

I think of the powerful little book *Power Through Prayer*, where E.M. Bounds wrote, "What the church needs today is not more machinery or better, not new organizations or more and novel methods, but men whom the Holy Ghost can use ... The Holy Ghost does not flow through methods, but through men ... He does not anoint plans, but men—men of prayer."

I agree. But I would add this: we need men and women who are given both to prayer and to proclamation, to seeking God for people and to seeking people for God.

In other words, we need models: people who go beyond the lowest-common-denominator approach of most methods to help believers share Christ effectively today. Jonathan Dodson is such a model. His writing on the gospel, both in explaining what it is and in describing how to show and share it, comes at a time when the church needs his mind, example, and heart.

When Paul recounted the powerful witness involved in establishing the church in Thessalonica, he said this: "We cared so much for you that we were pleased to share with you not only the gospel of God but also our own lives, because you had become dear to us" (1 Thessalonians 2:8, CSB). Our lonely, distrusting, and divided culture needs the gospel. People also need the kind of evangelism that involves us giving our own selves.

Yes, we can distill the good news down to a very simple tool, but what we need—and what those we seek to reach will be helped by—is more of our lives invested in the gospel and people, not less. We need to move from a little-as-possible witness to the sharing of our whole lives. You will find out how to do that in this book.

You will read about our search for beauty, as well as helpful metaphors to explain the gospel, and what Jonathan calls "shameless prayer." Bounds would have liked that phrase. Yes, there are actions steps—we need those. But we need more. Jonathan recognizes that we need help with having conversations that aren't immediately awkward for us or for those with whom we share.

I especially love Jonathan's phrase, "we talk about what we're taken with." Maybe this describes why we are in such a lull of personal evangelism in our day. Maybe we are taken with other things.

If you are ready to be taken with Jesus afresh—to be astonished at the wonder of Christ—keep reading. Your life and the lives of those you meet will be changed.

Ed Stetzer, Ph.D.
Talbot School of Theology, Biola University

1. TRUE WITNESS

"When I see a garden in flower, then I believe in God for a second. But not the rest of the time."
Svetlana Alexievich

When my British cousins visited us in Texas, we took them to the Fort Worth stockyards to give them a real Texas experience. The city is nicknamed "Cowtown" due to the millions of cows that cowboys drove through it along the Chisholm Trail in the mid-to-late 1800s. When the railroad arrived, Tetris-like, wooden cattle pens were created to funnel cows into 2,600 cattle stalls. But after the cattle industry dried up, some cattle pens were converted into a maze for tourists.

All eight of us paid the admission fee to enter the Cattlepen Maze, where the goal was to gather five punch holes in a scorecard and exit the maze as fast as you could. As I was gathering my punch holes, I crossed paths with various family members and asked them to point me to another punch-hole station. Sometimes they pointed me in the right direction; other times they tricked me by pointing me in the wrong direction!

Even after I gathered all the punch holes, I kept reaching dead ends in the maze. I began to end up in the same place where I had been before. I was lost. Anxiously searching for an emergency exit, I wondered if I would ever make it out of the maze. When I finally found the real exit, I breathed a sigh of relief, grateful for the "witnesses" who pointed me to the truth. And I won!

Most of us experience life like a giant maze. Sometimes our choices feel like an adventure. New experiences can be thrilling: falling in love, discovering insights through higher education, an intriguing career, inspiring world travel. But inevitably, the thrill wears off. A relationship dissolves, the career fizzles, disillusionment creeps in. A sense of lostness emerges. Will I ever find my way? How do I get out of this mess? Is there someone who can point me to the truth? We need real witnesses. Those who are spiritually lost need to hear from those who know the way, the truth, and the meaning of life. The world is desperate for true witnesses.

POINTING TO BEAUTY

Many people are searching for what is beautiful and true. The band Foster The People sing of feeling "lost without you" and being "lost in space" as they look for "signs of glowing afterlife." The song's lyrics suggest that our world is enchanted—embedded with neon-like signs that point to life after death. The psalms, too, remind us that creation glows with signs of "afterlife":

> *Bless the LORD, O my soul!*
> *O LORD my God, you are very great!*
> *You are clothed with splendor and majesty,*
> *covering yourself with light as with a garment,*
> *stretching out the heavens like a tent.*
> *He lays the beams of his chambers on the waters;*
> *he makes the clouds his chariot;*
> *he rides on the wings of the wind;*
> *he makes his messengers winds,*
> *his ministers a flaming fire. (Psalm 104:1-4)*

This psalm depicts divine *beauty* within creation. The brilliance of billions of stars in our galaxy are God's garment. The cosmos is depicted as a tent in which he chooses to dwell. His cosmic abode sits on the waters of the earth, and his vehicle leaps from cloud to cloud, carried on the wind of angelic wings. This is a poetic depiction of the beauty of God's grand home, but ultimately the universe is aflame with signs of *God's* glory. The wonders of the world beckon our attention to *his* splendor and majesty.

Beautiful things point beyond themselves to perfect beauty. Psalm 50 says, "Out of Zion, the perfection of beauty, God shines forth" (v 1). We're meant to trace the splendor of the world back to the sovereign one. One way in which we can bear witness to God is by *practicing beauty*. We practice beauty by making beautiful things, like writing lyrics that capture human longing, raising children with character, or planting a colorful garden.

I saw how effective this can be with my friend Ryan. Although Ryan had recently turned from skeptical unbelief to genuine faith in Jesus, he still had some doubts about Christianity. So I invited him to join me and our family for a road trip. We did the usual things: sang along to songs on the radio, corrected the kids when they got out of hand, ate some fast food.

The trip was pretty unremarkable to me, but years later Ryan shared with me how powerful it was for him to witness our children interacting with us in such a beautiful way. He was unaccustomed to the combination of respect and love that flowed freely within our family. His encounter with a family grounded in God's authority and love dealt a blow to his skepticism and strengthened his faith. Moms and dads, what you do matters, not only for your children but also for a watching world, which is admittedly wounded by broken parents.

Beauty can be found not only in the attractiveness of a tender family but also in a well-tended garden. Svetlana Alexievich is a Belarusian author who writes investigative, literary non-fiction depicting the bleak life of citizens of the Soviet Union. She conducted extensive research and countless interviews with sufferers to write *Secondhand*

Time: The Last of the Soviets.[1] In 2015, she was awarded the Nobel Prize for Literature for "her polyphonic writings, a monument to suffering and courage in our time."[2]

Her critique of oppressive regimes also resulted in her exile. Despite the pain of depicting great tragedy, or perhaps because of it, she writes, "When I see a garden in flower, then I believe in God for a second. But not the rest of the time."[3] Even someone who has suffered greatly and has documented unbelievable human anguish is provoked to believe *by the beauty* of a flower.

But why does beauty draw our attention? Because beauty bears witness to wholeness in a broken world. Beauty is a pledge of flourishing when things seem dire. The film *1917* follows two British soldiers during World War I on a mission to deliver a message that could save hundreds of lives. As they make their way across No Man's Land, their journey is filled with horror and punctuated by beauty.

The director, Sam Mendes, skillfully draws our attention to beauty in key moments in the film: a blossoming tree against a war-torn landscape, an act of kindness while on the run, soldiers singing amid the lament of great loss. Why does he introduce these aesthetic disruptions into the derelict landscape? Because beauty in our

---

[1] Svetlana Alexievich, *Secondhand Time: The Last of the Soviets* (Random House, 2017).

[2] The Nobel Prize in Literature 2015, nobelprize.org, Nobel Prize Outreach, December 18, 2024.

[3] Macha Gessen, "The Memory Keepers" *The New Yorker*, October 19, 2015.

broken world beckons belief in an unbroken, whole world. Loveliness suggests that things will not always be this bad.

If this is true, then those who possess the hope of the new creation should bear witness to this divine beauty. Plant beautiful gardens; cultivate families rooted in love and respect; write lyrics that capture hope; tend your life and mark out plots that may spark belief, even if only for a second. Who knows what God may do with it.

TELLING THE TRUTH

People are not only searching for beauty but also for where its glow comes from. Even if the beauty of character and creation suggest an afterlife, these witnesses are insufficient. Psalm 19 says, "Day to day pours out speech, and night to night reveals knowledge. There is no speech, nor are there words, whose voice is not heard" (v 2-3). Although creation speaks, it doesn't tell us everything we need to know.

Beauty may compel belief in God's existence, but only the good news can conjure saving faith. Dutch theologian Herman Bavinck writes, "Art in all its works and ways conjures up an ideal world before us ... But art cannot close the gulf between the ideal and the real. It cannot make the yonder of its vision the here of our present world."[4] So what bridges the gulf between ideal beauty and our gritty reality? How do we get the lyrics of creation into people's hands?

Through a witness. A true witness tells people where to go. She uses verbal testimony to get her point across. This is why Svetlana Alexievich's writing is so powerful. Her writing isn't a personal reflection on Soviet sufferers, but their *verbal witness* captured and transcribed to writing for us to read. When I was in the maze, beauty could not tell me how to escape. I needed a witness to tell me where to go in order to get out. How much more do the spiritually stranded need to hear a message of rescue? The lost need witnesses to tell them how to be found. Paul writes:

> *How then will they call on him in whom they have not believed? And how are they to believe in him of whom they have never heard? And how are they to hear without someone preaching? And how are they to preach unless they are sent? As it is written, "How beautiful are the feet of those who preach the good news!" (Romans 10:14-15)*

Almost daily someone will say to me, "Have you heard of so and so?" Very often, my answer is no. But in that moment, I am made aware of a person made in God's image that I never knew existed. Then that person will

---

[4] Herman Bavinck, *The Wonderful Works of God* (Westminster Seminary Press, 2024), p. 5.

elaborate on some quality about this stranger, and I learn about a good person. How much more do people need to hear about the greatest person that has ever walked the earth? Has something about Jesus struck you lately? Have you been surprised by his grace, encouraged by his forgiveness, struck by his beauty? Tell someone! When someone asks how you are doing, tell them about this great person.

Someone recently asked me how I was doing. Instead of giving them a pat answer, "Fine!" I told them the truth. Over the span of several weeks, I had contracted a painful case of the shingles, suffered a considerable financial setback, and lost my dear aunt to a heart attack. I was overwhelmed, my emotional capacity thin, and I felt like I was freefalling into despair.

I cried out to God and told him what I was feeling. I felt heard by God but still sad. I wrestled with dark thoughts all morning. Then I read Psalm 55:22: "Cast your burden on the LORD, and he will sustain you." The freefall stopped. I was buoyed by God's promise not only to shoulder my burdens but also to sustain me. I was reminded that all things are held together in Jesus (Colossians 1:17). In my despair, I encountered a great person who lifted me up, and I've been telling people about him all week.

Chatting with someone who confided in me that he had been depressed for weeks, I listened and empathized with him. Then, because I had experienced God's comforting promise, I was able to point him to the

God who promises to sustain us. I received a text from another person who confessed they were exhausted. When I shared the news about our burden-lifting God, they were immediately encouraged to trust Jesus.

Because the Scriptures bear witness to the truth, and I bore witness to others about Jesus, we experienced God's comforting grace. And that's what everyone needs to experience—but they can't if they don't hear about the person and promises of Jesus! We don't have to walk people through a whole gospel presentation or lead them through a Bible study. We can just describe an encounter with or a good quality of the greatest person we've ever met.

WE TALK ABOUT WHAT WE'RE TAKEN WITH

Hebrews describes Jesus as "the radiance of the glory of God and the exact imprint of his nature" (Hebrews 1:3). The Greek word for radiance only occurs this one time in the Bible. The author pulls it out for a special occasion. But what is radiance?

When we say to a bride on her wedding day, "You look radiant," what are we saying? You clean up nice? No, what we mean is she's *beautiful*. The radiance of the glory of God is the beauty of the person of Christ.

How do we respond to beautiful things? A fiery sunset, snowcapped peaks, a stunning painting, or a striking person? Do we agree or disagree with them? Do we inquire after their atomic composition? No, we *gaze* at them.

Gawk. Admire. Beauty is for beholding. We're made to behold the beauty of Christ—to gawk at his glory. Puritan theologian John Owen says, "One of the greatest privileges the believer has, both in this world and for eternity, is to behold the glory of Christ."[5] Why is beholding the glory of Christ one of the greatest privileges? Because Jesus is the exact imprint of God's nature.

The Greek word for imprint is *charakter*. Jesus Christ is the exact character of God. When we get our eyes checked, we sit down and look through a machine that alternates lenses until the perfect lens is found, making the letters on the eye chart crystal clear. Jesus Christ is the perfect lens, bringing God into focus. If you want to see God, look at Jesus. He is "very God of very God" as the Nicene Creed says. Jesus is *not* a forgery, a copy, or a knock-off. He is *divine* beauty.

So, to behold his glory is the privilege of all privileges. But how are we supposed to behold someone we can't see? We can observe the beauty of the mountains and the sun. Consider for a moment the reason why the mountains and the sun are there. Creation is meant not only to be seen but also to be seen through. Let me explain.

We used to live in a mansion on the North Shore of Boston (in the garage apartment) that faced the Atlantic Ocean. When the owners were gone, I would sneak

---

5 John Owen, abridged by R. J. K. Law, *The Glory of Christ* (Edinburgh: The Banner of Truth, 1994), p. 2.

into their living room and stand in front of two huge, gorgeous windows. But I didn't stare at the window frames or gawk at their size; I looked through the windows to soak in the expansive view of the Atlantic Ocean, the curling tail of Cape Cod, and the Boston skyline shooting up in the distance. I didn't look *at* the window; I looked *through* the window.

Similarly, we're meant to look not merely *at* creation but through it in order to apprehend the beauty of Christ. To trace the sunbeams back up to the radiance of the Son. To let our eyes climb up the mountains and off the peaks into the grandeur of Christ, through whom the world was made. Jesus is *the* beauty worth beholding—the glory worth gawking at.

Everyone talks about the things they love. If you see a movie you enjoy, you don't think to yourself, "I shouldn't tell anyone about this great movie." That would be weird. No, you tell people immediately. You announce the good news of a great film. If you loved the football game last night, you don't think, "I need to keep that news to myself." You blurt it out to your coworkers. "Did you see that pass?!" If you read a deeply satisfying novel, you tell others, "You should really read this book." We all talk about what we're taken with. If we're taken with Jesus, we will talk about Jesus.

The key to being a true witness is to be taken with the truth about Jesus. Many things distract our attention and call for our affections, but only one thing is worthy of all our attention and affection. Perhaps we would be more faithful gospel witnesses if we slowed down long enough to truly absorb the goodness and beauty of Jesus.

When I create space to reflect on my wife's incredible character, I find myself falling in love with her again. My thoughts drift to her kindhearted joy, her attentiveness to our three children, her strong work ethic, and her persistent grace with my stubborn sin, and I'm just taken with her all over again. Maybe you need to pause now and consider the beauty and kindness of Christ in your life, to find yourself taken with Jesus yet again.

A true witness shares the gospel with others, not only because it's true but also because it's beautiful news. The eternal Son of God, who could have judged us for our sin and unbelief, *chose* not merely to be judged but slain on our behalf. He did this out of great love for us, so that we can experience life-changing forgiveness and undying belonging, and enjoy eternal life with him. My goodness—that is good news!

But how do we faithfully express the gospel in the busyness of life? What does it look like to be a true witness in a city filled with what is false? Our next chapter explores what it means to be a *faithful presence* where God has placed us.

ACTION STEPS
- Think about your relationships, the gifts or resources God has given you, and the places

where he's planted you; how can you "practice beauty" in those areas to draw the attention of others to the Lord?

- Who were the people in your life that acted as true witnesses to bring you to faith in Jesus? Take a minute to thank God for them and send them a message of thanks too.

- Reflect on the things you are taken with. How could you cultivate being more taken with Jesus?

2. FAITHFUL PRESENCE

"Faithful presence calls believers to yield their will to God and to nurture and cultivate the world where God has placed them."
James Davidson Hunter

When I was doing mission work in Thailand each summer, I spoke the language as best as I could and greeted people with the *wai*—a slight bow with your palms pressed together. But no matter how well I executed the *wai*, or how pitch-perfect my speech was, I remained an outsider. The missionaries we worked alongside, however, were culturally accepted by the Thai people. How did these missionaries gain credibility? They became fluent in the language, moved into local neighborhoods, and in one case a missionary married a Thai wife. They became effective missionaries by embedding themselves in the local culture.

PUTTING DOWN ROOTS

According to the US Census Bureau, Americans move on average 11.7 times in their lifetime.[6] Globally, cities in particular are hotbeds of migration. It's hard for Christians to be effective missionaries when they don't have roots in a community. On the other hand, living in one place isn't sufficient for gospel witness if we never engage with our neighbors. You can be a committed suburbanite and avoid your neighbors your entire life. You can live in a small town, know just about everyone by name, and never share the good news with them. To be faithful missionaries, we have to practice a certain kind of *presence*.

When the people of Israel were sent into exile in Babylon, the prophet Jeremiah wrote them a set of instructions on how to live in a religiously hostile and culturally foreign land. He wrote, "Build houses and live in them; plant gardens and eat their produce. Take wives and have sons and daughters; take wives for your sons, and give your daughters in marriage, that they may bear sons and daughters; multiply there, and do not decrease" (Jeremiah 29:5-6). Jeremiah's counsel carries three key concepts that help us understand what it means to be a missional people: faithful presence, frequent prayer, and full-orbed *shalom*. Let's take a look at the first of these.

---

6 "Calculating Migration Expectancy Using ACS Data," https://www.census.gov/topics/population/migration/guidance/calculating-migration-expectancy.html (accessed December 2024).

FAITHFUL PRESENCE

Jeremiah counseled God's people not to see life in Babylon as a temporary punishment but as a missionary assignment. Is that how you see your neighborhood? Your city? This counsel would have been shocking to the exiles. The Babylonians had conquered, killed, and taken captive Israelites. The Israelites were forced to live in the heart of enemy territory. As a result, some false prophets told these Jewish exiles that their exile would only last a couple of years and advised them not to get comfortable in Babylon (27:14 – 28:4). But Jeremiah challenged the false prophecy by insisting their exile would be 70 years (29:10). He instructed them to build houses, plant gardens, and produce generations to *bless* their enemies. It turns out that Jeremiah was the divinely authorized prophet.

SOCIAL, CULTURAL, AND SPIRITUAL BLESSING

How did the exiles live in Babylon? Jeremiah counseled them to be an *economic* blessing: to plant gardens and eat their produce, not simply to live off the toil of the Babylonians. He also instructed them to be a *social* blessing: to build their own houses and live in them, not to squeeze into the existing infrastructure. They were to marry, have children, and settle in, living in a way that blessed their enemies. These instructions sound very similar to those of Jesus: "Love your enemies, do what is good to those who hate you, bless those who curse you, pray for those who mistreat you" (Luke 6:27-28, HCSB).

What might it look like for you to be an economic blessing to your neighbors? It could be simple things—for example, working hard and ethically or living within your means and tipping generously. My wife used to be a waitress at a major restaurant chain. She dreaded Sundays because the church crowd were the worst tippers. One regular customer would faithfully leave a gospel tract on the table and no tip.

What if we tipped in light of God's generosity toward us? What if the church crowd became the most desirable crowd to have at a restaurant? We would be an economic blessing to struggling waitstaff and pique their interest in the God we serve! We can also be an economic blessing by hiring people, supporting non-profits that help the unemployed, and tithing to churches that meet physical and social needs.

Jeremiah also tells God's people to be a *spiritual* blessing to their captors by seeking the welfare of the city: "But seek the welfare of the city where I have sent you into exile, and pray to the LORD on its behalf" (Jeremiah 29:7). The word "welfare" comes from the Hebrew word *shalom*, which refers to whole-person flourishing. Notice that they prayed for the city and sought the welfare of their enemies. How would your prayers change if you included your political opponents in them? Are there people who have hurt you that you can bring God's grace over? What might it look like for you to seek the good of those around you?

Unfortunately, some Christians today are deceived and listen to the wrong voices, just like the exiles followed the advice of the false prophets: "Do not let your prophets and your diviners who are among you deceive you, and do not listen to the dreams that they dream, for it is a lie that they are prophesying to you in my name; I did not send them, declares the LORD" (v 8-9). It can be tempting to become insular and withdraw from society, especially in times of moral decline. But withdrawal doesn't make us holy, and it definitely doesn't make others holy. Jesus was the holiest person who ever walked the planet, and he frequently hung out with sinners. While the concern for personal holiness is commendable, we need to recognize that personal morality is only one aspect of sanctified living. Desiring *shalom* for all people is also an act of holiness, and it should compel us to seek the good of those around us with gospel hope.

Perhaps you're thinking, "If we spend time with sinners, how do we remain holy? Aren't we supposed to be distinct from the world?" After all, while we too are sinners, we are called to live a holy life. Israel had been forced from the temple at Jerusalem, but they created the synagogue in Babylon. Synagogues functioned as satellite temples, where the exiles could learn the Torah, pray, gather as a community, and worship. So, while they were engaged in the city, they also remained distinct from it by prioritizing worship of the one true God. They lived distinctive lives marked by holiness by maintaining a *devotional* presence. Synagogue life reinforced their devotion to God, which in turn compelled them to be a blessing to those around them.

Our personal holiness is also a blessing to society. Husbands and wives who practice sexual and emotional fidelity to one another and do not commit adultery create stable bonds in which children thrive.[7] Individuals who don't participate in pornography but cultivate sexual integrity stymie the rampant sex-trafficking industry.[8] Employees who work with integrity create healthy work environments and often increase a company's bottom line.[9] Righteousness matters not only to God but also to society.

A devotional presence enabled God's people to seek the welfare of the city without being sucked into its idolatrous ways, making Israel a spiritually vibrant presence in Babylon. Ideally, God's people weren't to simply blend into the dominant culture. Instead, they became what sociologist James Davison Hunter calls a "faithful presence."[10] Faithful to what? Not foremost to the city—that would have given them a savior complex, making them feel like it was their responsibility to solve

---

[7] According to the Heritage Foundation, married people are less likely to experience depression, and marriage reduces the probability of child poverty by 80%. See: https://www.heritage.org/marriage-and-family/heritage-explains/why-the-declining-marriage-rate-affects-everyone# (accessed December 2024).

[8] Research indicates that consumption of pornography correlates with a higher likelihood of buying sex, bullying, and sexual violence. See P J Wright, R.S. Tokunaga, & A Kraus, "A meta-analysis of pornography consumption and actual acts of sexual aggression in general population studies," *Journal of Communication*, 2016 66(1), p. 183-205.

[9] See: https://www.inc.com/peter-cohan/how-integrity-boosts-your-bottom-line.html

[10] James Davison Hunter, *To Change the World* (Oxford University Press, 2010), p. 234-254.

all the problems of Babylon. They were faithful to God, who empowered them to be faithful to the deep and complex needs of those around them.

Similarly, the church is called to be a faithful presence in the world. In robust faithfulness to God, we seek the welfare of our towns and cities: economically, socially, culturally, and spiritually. This type of living can be seen in the lives of families like the Talberts. When they moved into a new neighborhood, they got to know their neighbors, arranged play dates, and hosted parties. Over time they got to know Betty, a hoarder who lived in squalor next door. The Talberts befriended her, helped her clean out her house, assisted her with rent, and regularly took her to get groceries. When asked why they did all this, they pointed to Jesus, who put on flesh and moved into the neighborhood (John 1:14, MSG). The Talberts' neighbors knew they could turn to them when they needed help. Is that true of your neighbors? If you moved away, would anyone notice?

PRACTICING FAITHFUL PRESENCE
How can we be a faithful presence in our own context? Here are some practical ways to seek the shalom of your neighbors:

Socially
- Walk in your neighborhood and chat with your neighbors.
- Invite neighbors over for dinner and parties.

- Cut the grass, walk the dog, and take out trash for neighbors who are out of town.
- Arrange a neighbor meetup or street party.
- Attend a happy hour with people in your apartment complex.
- Participate in local holiday celebrations in your neighborhood or condos.

Economically
- Support local businesses and tip those who serve you generously.
- Brighten your coworkers' lives by giving them encouragement.
- Do your job with excellence and integrity.
- Use your finances to contribute to non-profits and church ministry.
- Pay your taxes.
- Pray for your coworkers.
- Create new jobs through entrepreneurial efforts.
- Be generous with your money and possessions.

Culturally
- Support local artists by attending concerts and buying local art.

- Follow and praise local artists on social media.
- Read local publications and look for bits of truth, beauty, and goodness.
- Volunteer in your local schools.
- Attend town or city hall meetings and participate in local elections.
- Join groups for hobbies you enjoy to meet new people in your area (for example, ultimate frisbee, book clubs, knitting, woodworking).

Spiritually
- Respectfully inquire about other people's worldviews.
- Regularly worship with your church.
- Pray for your neighbors by name and ask God for their salvation.
- Pray for social, economic, and cultural issues.
- Share the gospel in personal, engaging ways with non-Christians.
- Ask for the Spirit's leading in your life.

We live in our homes not by accident but by providence. Jeremiah tells the exiles twice that it was God, not Nebuchadnezzar, who sent them into exile: "Thus says the LORD of hosts, the God of Israel, to all the exiles whom I have sent into exile from Jerusalem to Babylon" (Jeremiah 29:4, 7). Similarly, we have been sent as exiles into this world to proclaim the excellencies of God (1 Peter 2:11-12; Hebrews 11:13).

Our mission is to be faithfully present in our neighborhoods, apartments, and condos. As Paul says, "And he made from one man every nation of mankind to live on all the face of the earth, having determined allotted periods and the boundaries of their dwelling place, that they should seek God, and perhaps feel their way toward him and find him" (Acts 17:26-27). Our times and places, seasons of life, and living places have been appointed by God so that others can find him. Let's make the church crowd a beloved crowd.

FREQUENT PRAYER

A second way Jeremiah instructs the exiles to seek the welfare of the city is through prayer: "But seek the welfare of the city where I have sent you into exile, and *pray to the LORD on its behalf*" (Jeremiah 29:7). This would have been a shocking request to the Israelites. God was asking them to pray for the people who had ripped them from their homes, destroyed their land, desecrated their temple and blinded their king, and who sought to assimilate them into their culture and religion. Yet God urges them to do good to those who hate them. When we feel marginalized or out of place in our culture, it can be tempting to despise or smear those who disagree with us. But Jeremiah counsels us to pray for them. Wherever the city is darkest is where the light can shine the brightest.

PRAY ON SITE WITH INSIGHT

How can we practice praying regularly for those around us? Missiologist Steve Hawthorne encourages us to "pray on site with insight."[11] As you walk around the neighborhood, commute into the city, or drive through the suburbs, allow the sights you see to inform your prayers. When I see our skyline, I frequently say aloud, "Lord, renew this city." When you pass government buildings, ask the Lord to give your elected officials wisdom for the flourishing of the city and wider area. If you drive by shopping malls, ask the Lord to make true worshipers out of devoted consumers. Pray that God disentangles your neighbors from the idols of the city.

In addition, thank God for the positive things you see in your city, asking him to strengthen those areas. When you pass by places of commerce, pray for businesses to flourish, work culture to be healthy, and the economy to thrive. Thank God for green spaces, truthful and beautiful public art, music venues, theaters, and all who show us the beauty of our great God. I recently visited a friend at his workplace, and while I was there, he called his team together and led them in prayer, asking for wisdom for his team and healing for the patients they

---

11 Steve Hawthorne and Graham Kendrick, *Prayer-Walking: Praying on Site with Insight* (Charisma House, 1996), p. 12.

attend to. If your workplace permits it, pray on the spot, not just off-site! Look for opportunities to pray with a hurting coworker or a struggling neighbor. Your time and place have been appointed by God so that others might reach out and find him.

We can also participate in corporate prayer with our roommates, families, small groups, and churches. Ask God to bring spiritual awakening, human flourishing, and transformation in your home. Our church participates in monthly prayer for the city. We invite church members to sign up for 30-minute slots every second Thursday of the month to cover a whole day in prayer for our city. If your church doesn't do that, you can put it in your personal calendar to pray every second Thursday of the month, or whatever regular slot suits you, for God to renew your area socially, spiritually, and culturally with the gospel of Jesus.

STAY CLOSE TO GOD

If we seek the welfare of the city *apart from prayer,* we will quickly tire out, become disillusioned, and collapse into apathy when we don't see the results we want. Or we will become arrogant, self-congratulating, and triumphalist when we do see results. Prayer places us underneath God's providence and in his power. In prayer, we learn to trust God's timing and experience his transformation. Faithful praying forms us. When we stay close to the Lord in prayer, we begin to see others as Jesus does: "harassed and helpless, like sheep without a shepherd"

(Matthew 9:36). Jesus' compassion transforms us into a faithful presence.

When cyclists draft behind another cyclist, they position themselves inches behind the rider to stay in their slipstream. This reduces headwind and increases speed by up to 5 miles (8km) an hour. But when a cyclist falls out of the slipstream, they have to exert a lot of effort to catch up, which cyclists call "burning a match." When we pray, we draft God's power and trust God's providence. He carries us through everyday challenges and the difficulties of being a faithful presence. But if you fall out of God's draft, be encouraged—you don't have to burn a match to get back. Just turn around, face Jesus, confess your sins, and receive his grace immediately, for he is faithfully present, always, especially when we are faithless.

FULL-ORBED SHALOM

A third way to live as exiles is to seek the peace of the city: "But seek the welfare of the city where I have sent you into exile, and pray to the LORD on its behalf, for in its welfare you will find your welfare" (Jeremiah 29:7). When we hear the word "welfare" today, we think of government programs and handouts, but those are just facets of biblical welfare. The Hebrew word *shalom* is much more robust. It can be translated "welfare" or "peace," but those words fall short of the full meaning of shalom. Shalom is multifaceted—a full-orbed, all-encompassing healing of what is broken.

Shalom isn't merely the cessation of war but the presence of peace: not just a lower crime rate but opportunities for those marginalized by crime. It is human flourishing because of faithful, godly presence. Theologian Cornelius Plantinga Jr. describes shalom as "the webbing together of God, humans and all creation in justice, fulfillment, and delight."[12] It's a vision of the world that we all want but only Christ can guarantee (Isaiah 60 – 61; Revelation 21 – 22).

How might we go about seeking the shalom of the city? Remember Jeremiah's call to plant and build? Planting began in Eden, where God planted the garden and called Adam and Eve to cultivate it. We seek the shalom of the city through faithful presence in our *vocation*. It's balancing spreadsheets to represent true values; raising children who serve (not just use) the city; treating disagreeable coworkers with love, and political opposites with dignity; it's teaching, creating, and designing in goodness, truth, and beauty, all out of devotion to God.

Another way to express this shalom is to seek *reconciliation* in relationships. Since we have been reconciled to God through Jesus, who made peace by the blood of his cross (Colossians 1:10), we can extend forgiveness and seek peace in conflict. A Christian should be the first to apologize for error or wrongdoing and seek reconciliation in the work place. Christian

---

[12] Cornelius Plantinga Jr., *Not the Way It's Supposed to Be: A Breviary of Sin* (Eerdmans, 1996), p. 10.

marriages will not be perfect, but we get to showcase the forgiveness of God in keeping short accounts with one another and seeking marital peace. When our unbelieving world sees this countercultural forgiveness and peace-seeking in action, they see a demonstration of the uniqueness of the gospel.

We also seek the good of the city through *evangelism* by inviting people into the heart of shalom— introducing them to Jesus Christ, who did not remain in heaven but came to earth to endure exile on behalf of sinners under God's wrath, in his life, death, and resurrection. We will focus on gospel witness in the next few chapters, but consider first the Christ who is *the* faithful presence, who succeeded where we failed. He is the second Adam, who knits humans, creation, justice, and delight all back together with God through his renewing grace. People need to hear about *this* Jesus.

Too often our gospel is reduced to nothing more than a spiritual transaction: you are a sinner; Jesus is the Savior. Repent and believe in him, and you will be saved. While all that is true, Jesus died and rose to accomplish much more than only a spiritual transaction. Colossians tells us that he reconciles *all things*, in heaven and on earth, *"making peace* by the blood of his cross" (Colossians 1:20). Jesus is after full-orbed shalom. He died and rose to heal hearts, relationships, societies, injustices, nations, the world. What if we told the world that this future is promised to us through faith in Jesus?

Like a cyclist, let's stay in the draft of Christ. Allow him to carry us not only into forgiveness but into the hope of the promised whole new creation. Let's practice a faithful presence and proclaim the full gospel that draws people to the way, the truth and the life.

ACTION STEPS

- If you were absent from your community and/or workplace, how would your absence be felt? If you can't think of something, you may want to take a few minutes to pray about why this might be and what could change.

- In which area is the Spirit prompting some reform in your life: calling you to practice a faithful economic, social, or spiritual presence? Write down a couple of ways you can be obedient to him, and share this with someone else.

- Could you get involved in any church activities for the community or join a group based on one of your hobbies to get to know local people?

3. IMPLAUSIBLE EVANGELISM

"If you believe in Jesus's message, you believe in a truth, but not a truth that leads to exclusion ... The real issue is, then, which kind of truth—and which kind of identity that the truth produces—leads you to embrace people who are deeply different from you?"
Tim Keller

Not everyone welcomes the good news of Jesus Christ. According to the U.S. Commission on International Religious Freedom, there are 46 countries that maintain some kind of anti-conversion law.[13] And even where evangelism is legal, we're often encouraged

---

13 The commission distinguishes between four types of anti-conversion laws: anti-proselytism laws, interfaith marriage laws, apostasy laws, and identity documentation laws. See the "Anti-Conversion Laws Compendium," https://www.govinfo.gov/content/pkg/GOVPUB-Y3_R27-PURL-gpo224105/pdf/GOVPUB-Y3_R27-PURL-gpo224105.pdf (accessed December 2024).

by our society to identify with whatever we want and to find "what's true for you." With so many possible things to identify with, why should people find their identity in Christ? Moreover, many Christians prefer to let their actions do the talking instead of giving verbal witness to the person and work of Jesus. All of these issues raise an important question: is evangelism even plausible?

DEFINING EVANGELISM

Before considering evangelism in our modern age, it's important to establish what evangelism is. Missiologist David Bosch defines evangelism as "the core, heart, or center of mission: it consists in the proclamation of salvation in Christ to nonbelievers, in announcing forgiveness of sins, in calling people to repentance and faith in Christ, in inviting them to become living members of Christ's earthly community and to begin a life in the power of the Spirit."[14]

There's a lot to his definition, but notice first that Bosch describes evangelism in *verbal* terms: proclaiming, announcing, and inviting. Jesus himself began his ministry by proclaiming the gospel and calling people to repentance: "Now after John was arrested, Jesus came into Galilee, *proclaiming* the gospel of God, and

---

14 David Bosch, "Evangelism: Theological Currents and Cross-Currents Today," in *The Study of Evangelism: Exploring a Missional Practice of the Church* (ed. Paul W. Chilcote and Laceye C. Warner), (Eerdmans, 2008), p. 9. I further explore Bosch's definition in my book on evangelism, *The Unbelievable Gospel: Say Something Worth Believing* (Zondervan, 2014), p. 26-29.

saying, 'The time is fulfilled, and the kingdom of God is at hand; repent and believe in the gospel'" (Mark 1:14-15).

Jesus modeled evangelism by proclaiming the gospel, but he didn't restrict evangelism to himself. He mentored his disciples in evangelism throughout his ministry: "And he appointed twelve (whom he also named apostles) so that they might be with him and he might send them out to preach and have authority to cast out demons" (3:14-15). Notice that one of the reasons why Jesus appointed the apostles was to send them out *to preach*. But their ministry wasn't only done with life-altering words; they also cast out demons to deliver people from oppression. Their evangelistic ministry combined words and deeds, gospel proclamation and demonstration, as the kingdom of God broke into their communities.

This kingdom-coming gospel ministry isn't reserved for the apostles. Jesus includes us in his evangelistic ministry by commissioning the church to maintain the "center of mission" through gospel witness: "Go into all the world and proclaim the gospel to the whole creation. Whoever believes and is baptized will be saved, but whoever does not believe will be condemned" (16:15-16). This is the greatest mission on earth—soul-saving, kingdom-coming, creation-restoring work! But given all the resistance to the gospel, is evangelism even plausible?

IS EVANGELISM PLAUSIBLE?

It's remarkable that Jesus includes us in his grand mission for the world. Yet we often lose sight of this privilege. It's easy to get bogged down in our own responsibilities or troubles and be unaware of what God is doing in the world. Alternatively, we may feel hesitant to share the gospel for a number of reasons.

Social Distance

During the months of Covid lockdowns, I had very little interaction with non-Christians. When I went for my morning walk, neighbors crossed the street to avoid making contact with me. When we celebrated my daughter's birthday, her friends drove by our condo and honked their horns: no hugs, no laughs, no blowing out candles with friends.

Although epidemiologists later described this phenomenon more correctly as "physical distancing," it was too late—the world was accustomed to the term *social* distancing. Fear of contracting a life-threatening virus disrupted the social fabric of the world. Months later, after Covid protocols were lifted, many struggled to return to ordinary patterns of social interaction.

During the pandemic, our family moved into a new neighborhood. Unlike living in our previous neighborhoods, we really struggled to connect with our neighbors. There were a lot of reasons for this. Our neighbors were adjusting to social anxiety, new social patterns, and working from home. We also struggled to connect because of our selfish indifference and our stage of life. But bottom line, I had very few relationships with non-Christians.

Being a faithful presence is an important part of evangelism. If we're not engaging with people in the ebb and flow of ordinary social interactions, it becomes awkward and difficult to share the gospel with people who desperately need it. When the various strands of commerce, arts and entertainment, neighborhood life, office space, and fitness become isolated, it makes it much harder to be faithfully present in our communities. And if we aren't deliberate, the Covid legacy will remain in our lives instead, restricting our engagement with coworkers, grocers, baristas, colleagues, gym or sports-club members, and neighbors—who desperately need to hear the good news.

Cultural Resistance
Social distance isn't the only obstacle to sharing our faith. Very often we encounter what Abraham Kuyper described as a spiritual "antithesis" between those who are committed to the kingdom of God and those who have a negative cultural disposition toward Christianity.[15] This antithesis exists for some good reasons.

We had just moved to America's oldest seaport, Gloucester, Massachusetts, when I heard a rap on the door. I opened

---

15 James D. Bratt, ed., *Abraham Kuyper: A Centennial Reader* (Eerdmans, 1998), p. 15.

it to see a couple of people who introduced themselves with big smiles and asked me if I believed in God and if I wanted to talk. I invited them in for a chat. As we talked, I felt uneasy. Beneath the veneer of kindness, I could feel a pressure to cave in to their beliefs. They urged me to read their literature, a magazine with apocalyptic images on the cover. When I challenged some of their beliefs, they became forceful. My sense of unease morphed into distaste as the Jehovah's Witnesses tried to convert me to their religion.

Many people feel a similar unease about Christians who evangelize. They perceive evangelism as a way for religious people to dominate others with their doctrinal beliefs or to fill a spiritual quota. In order to distinguish ourselves from cultic proselytizers, it is important to sympathize with the secular experience of evangelism. Moreover, we have every reason to be disarming when we talk about Jesus, since conversion isn't our job. There is only one effective evangelist, and his name is the Holy Spirit.

When we embrace this reality, we will converse about the gospel in a way that is more natural, winsome, and true, and less forced and coercive. While many religious people are fanatical and coercive in their beliefs, Jesus had a non-oppressive approach to evangelism. That doesn't mean he never debated or encountered rejection, but it does mean that he was able to talk about his beliefs in a respectful way. (For example, Mark 10:17-22; John 3:1-15; 4:1-29.)

Spiritual Resistance

We also face spiritual resistance to the good news. Scripture describes humans as being "stiff-necked" (Acts 7:51), possessing "a heart of stone" (Ezekiel 11:19), and as natural born "enemies" of God (Romans 5:10). Paul writes, "They are gossips, slanderers, haters of God, insolent, haughty, boastful, inventors of evil, disobedient to parents, foolish, faithless, heartless, ruthless" (Romans 1:29-31). This is an offensive description of humanity. We may be tempted to object: *I don't see this resistance in all people. Is this really true of everyone?*

This list combines disposition with actions. While we may not witness some of these depraved actions in one another, we all possess the disposition of faithless hatred toward God. We are born into this world loving ourselves instead of loving God. As Romans 1 describes it, we "exchanged the truth about God for a lie and worshiped and served the creature rather than the Creator" (v 25). Everyone naturally seeks their own interest over the interests of God. We adore ourselves instead of our Creator, and we stubbornly insist on living for ourselves, apart from the intervening grace of God.

Since we are spiritually resistant to God, we desperately need something to dismantle our defenses. The good character of Christians and the beauty of creation are inadequate for that. We need a new conscience and "a heart of flesh" to become friends with God. We need to be born again.

The notion of being born a second time is strange, but we often use this image to explain new experiences. When launching a new initiative we might say, "We birthed a new program!" Or reflecting on a first date, we may declare, "That's when our relationship was born!" In fact, a second birth is associated with tremendous joy and hope.

In 2006, a paper was published in the *Journal of Psychopharmacology* which tracked the experiences of participants who took psilocybin (aka magic mushrooms).[16] Each participant took this drug in a controlled environment. Afterwards, they described their drug-induced state as "one of the most spiritually significant experiences of their lives," comparing it to the birth of a first child. But the new birth that God offers to humanity is the most significant spiritual experience available to humanity. It grants us a new identity and a sense of belonging, and it reconciles us with our beneficent Creator to enjoy his perfect love. No drug can accomplish that. But how is a person spiritually reborn?

The apostle Peter says we can be born again by an imperishable seed through the living word of God (1 Peter 1:23). Hard hearts don't become soft without gospel seed entering them. Dead enemies of God don't become his

---

[16] Michael Pollan, *How to Change Your Mind: What the New Science of Psychedelics Teaches Us About Consciousness, Dying, Addiction, Depression, and Transcendence* (Penguin, 2018), p. 11.

communicates the truth of the gospel. Although the treasure is eternally secure in heaven, it breaks into the present when we surrender to Jesus. If the rich man will follow Jesus, he will obtain the inexhaustible riches of Christ himself.

I was recently picked up by a Lyft driver. When I got into the car, I noticed he had an accent, and I asked where he was from. He told me he was from Ukraine. This was during Russia's invasion of Ukraine, so I offered my sympathies for the devastating toll the war has taken on his people. As we talked, it became apparent that the humanitarian crisis in his country was heavy on his heart. He told me that his parents still live there, and when he calls them, he can hear bombs in the background and airplanes flying overhead.

As I asked him more questions, the driver spoke at length about the politics of the war and the evil atrocities. He wanted justice and peace. I asked him how he copes with the evil. He turned the question back on me, so I described Jesus as the "Prince of Peace" (Isaiah 9:6) and what he did on the cross to absorb evil and put it on notice. Jesus will establish justice once and for all when he returns. I asked him if he knew Jesus and encouraged him to trust the Prince of Peace.

Finally, I asked if I could pray for him, his family, and his country. After I prayed for him, he was visibly moved and thanked me, and I got out of the car. I was able to share the gospel with this Lyft driver by asking questions, listening, focusing on the heart, and sharing the good news through an idea that chimed with what was near to his heart—the Prince of Peace.

What have we learned about evangelism from Jesus? By listening, asking questions, focusing on the heart, and speaking through a gospel metaphor, we can effectively and personally share the gospel with others. We will elaborate on how to use gospel metaphors in the next chapter. But for now, the next time you are conversing with one of your lost family members or secular friends, try following Jesus into the conversation by asking questions, picking up on the language of the heart, and looking for a metaphor or idea that might be most meaningful or relevant to them.

Try to discern the one thing they are unwilling to give up. For example, if it is sexual pleasure, perhaps share how Christ satisfies the heart. If it is acceptance from others, tell them how they can be perfectly accepted by God in Christ. As you listen to others, ask the Spirit to help you discern the one thing they are unwilling to surrender and how Jesus perfectly takes its place.

PAUL'S EVANGELISTIC ADVICE

Jesus' disciple, the apostle Paul, was also a discerning evangelist. He counseled the Colossians, "Walk in wisdom toward outsiders, making the best use of the time. Let your speech always be gracious, seasoned with salt, so that you may know how you ought to answer each person" (Colossians 4:5-6). Three things stand out from his instruction: walk in wisdom; always be gracious; answer each person.

Walk in Wisdom

What does the wise person look like? In his book *How to Know a Person*, David Brooks says, "Wise people don't tell you what to do; they help you process your own thoughts and emotions. They enter with you into your process of meaning-making and then help you expand it, push it along."[19] A wise evangelist listens to others closely to discern how they can best help them move toward Christ. A wise person doesn't run over people with arguments but walks toward them in discernment. A wise person considers the obstacles and objections an outsider to Christianity may have, and tries to see things from their point of view, so they can speak a word of grace into their lives.

One way to walk wisely toward those outside the faith is to identify with their struggles or unbelief. While they may be on the outside of Christ, those of us on the inside need Jesus just as much. Unfortunately, we often project the opposite idea. Instead of trying to convert people to the gospel, consider showing them your need for the gospel.

I was chatting with a skeptic who was struggling with the big questions of life. He said, "Jonathan, do you ever

---

19 David Brooks, *How to Know a Person* (Random House, 2023), p. 249.

doubt?" I replied, "Well, it depends on what you mean by doubt. I don't doubt the basic claims of Christ, but I do struggle with unbelief." He tilted his head and looked at me quizzically. I explained to him what I had been putting my worth in. Earlier in the day, I had posted something on Twitter that I thought was pretty insightful. I checked an hour later, and no one had retweeted it. I checked again, and still no comment. Then again: no like, no retweet, nothing. My heart sank.

Why did my heart sink? Because I believed the approval of the anonymous Twittersphere was more valuable than the approval of God in Christ. I exchanged Jesus' perfect approval for the fleeting approval of strangers. But I confessed my sin to Jesus, and he reaffirmed his forgiving, accepting love in my heart, which drove out my insecurity. Instead of projecting the image of a doubt-free, Bible-answer man, I let my friend in on my current need for Jesus. I didn't imagine myself as better but showed myself as his equal: a fellow struggler also in need of God's perfect love in Christ.

Gracious Speech
What does gracious speech look like? It is seasoned with salt. It has variety and life. It is interesting and engaging. This person avoids pat answers and canned responses. Paul is describing a person who is deeply interested in others—their lives, jobs, hobbies, relationships, hopes, fears, and beliefs—and asks questions. This person isn't poised to condemn, nor are they afraid to speak; they are

living friends apart from hearing the living word of God. We cannot escape the bad news of self-worship without hearing the good news of the gospel: Jesus' death for our sin and his resurrection for our new life. Peter concludes, "And this word is the good news that was preached to you" (v 25). The only way for the spiritually resistant to be liberated into the saving love of Jesus Christ is for someone to preach the gospel to them. Spiritual death and resistance can be overturned by a single, eternal, powerful word shared by an ordinary Christian.

So, is evangelism plausible? Yes, in fact it is essential. No one gets in on new life in Christ apart from hearing the good news. Our friends, family members, and neighbors are stranded in a Christless eternity apart from hearing about Jesus. How then should we go about sharing the gospel? Let's consider Jesus' unique approach to evangelism.

COMPASSIONATE EVANGELISM

What makes Jesus' evangelism different? One difference is his motivation. As he traveled from city to city, preaching and teaching the gospel, we learn that Jesus evangelized with compassion, not coercion: "When he saw the crowds, he had compassion for them, because they were harassed and helpless, like sheep without a shepherd" (Matthew 9:36). The word "compassion" comes from the Greek word *splanchnizomai*, which means "from the bowels." Today we might say, "He felt it in the gut." This means Jesus wasn't motivated by a surface emotion but a deep-seated concern for others. He wasn't just trying to fill an evangelistic quota of converts; he actually cared deeply for those he preached to. Jesus looked out on the mass of people made in his image and *felt* for them. Do you feel *splanchnizomai* for those around you? Or do you see them as projects to complete or perhaps persons to avoid?

Why did Jesus feel such great compassion for the crowds? Because they were "harassed and helpless." These two words can be translated "mangled and thrown to the ground." They are oppressive words. Why were the people so oppressed? Probably for a combination of reasons. The Jews were under the oppressive rule of the Romans, who were forcing their pagan beliefs and culture onto the Jewish way of life. But the Pharisees were also oppressing their people with excessive, burdensome laws which were added on top of the Old Testament laws.

Jesus sees the people before him as beat up, extorted, and abused by Roman ideology—the *Pax Romana* (the peace of Rome), which offered very little real peace. Moved by their plight, Jesus preaches the good news of true peace. He shares a gospel that lifts the burdens of law-keeping perfectionism and oppressive ideology. Unlike Rome, he doesn't look at the multitudes as sheep to be slaughtered or dominated but as sheep without a shepherd to care for them and guide them.

Jesus' evangelism is different not only because he is compassionate but because he preaches a message that relieves guilt instead of compounding guilt. The gospel lifts burdens. Jesus is exemplary in both his motivation and his message. He demonstrates that evangelism is not only plausible but *considerate*.

THE MODERN SELF

We too should be motivated by compassion. Today, our fellow citizens are unknowingly dominated by forces that mangle and throw them to the ground. One lingering force is the ideology of the modern self. The modern self is akin to superman. It is autonomous and decisive. Like Captain Nemo of *20,000 Leagues Under the Sea*, it is the captain of the ship, braving new worlds in underwater paradise, utterly self-reliant.

This self-reliant, self-centered spirit was sparked by the Renaissance, which led to some positive things like liberal democracy instead of oppressive monarchies, but it also led to injustices like colonialism—exploitation of other countries for wealth and land. As hundreds of years went by, postmodern philosophers of the late 20th century rejected this idea of the autonomous self, calling it a modern fiction. They exposed the dark side of the modern person, pulling the rug out from under our feet by saying that there is no true self. Heroes turned into anti-heroes: the Dark Knight instead of Batman; Catwoman instead of Superwoman. In this opposing view, everything is morally gray; there is no fixed truth—no fixed identity. And the bottom dropped out. The center did not hold. Identity went from confident to doubting—from assertive to divided. In this prevailing social narrative, we have been inundated with many possible identities, causing confusion.

MANY IDENTITIES

Without a fixed sense of self, life is a masquerade ball. We change masks many times a day. To some, we are the risky party animal; to others, the successful professional; the doting mother; the hip single; the thoughtful reader; the indie music aficionado; the caring husband; the justice crusader; the social-media influencer; the pietistic Christian; the fashion icon; the start-up genius, and on and on. We subtly believe, *There is no essential me; I can become whoever I construct myself to be.*

Life becomes a carnival: fun, distracting, and constantly changing. We reinvent gender, sex, and ourselves. Olympian Bruce Jenner declared his soul was female and chose to identify as a woman. This public transformation of self was a key moment in an avalanche of transgenderism. This generation is tempted to find meaning in many identities. But eventually the excitement of the masquerade ball loses its luster, and the late modern age is becoming marked by record anxiety. Confused, hopeless, mangled, and thrown to the ground, the late modern self is in a crisis.

The band Broken Bells captures this lostness well when they sing about a decentered self stumbling through what looks like a liberating open door into a lost state in their song "Perfect World". It turns out that the many-selved quest leaves us unfulfilled and "wanting more"—it's been a lie for so long that, as their lyrics attest, we don't even know we are faking. People are lost, hurting, confused, and unfulfilled. They are in desperate need of compassionate evangelists who will lovingly tell them about the hope of a fixed identity as a redeemed child of God. Will you have compassion on the multitudes? Will you point them to the hope of becoming a new creation?

EVANGELISM OFFERS A BETTER IDENTITY

When Jesus saw sheep without a shepherd, he did not leave them to fend for themselves. He was already responding by "teaching in their synagogues and proclaiming the gospel of the kingdom and healing every disease and every affliction" (Matthew 9:35). Jesus reacted to the lostness of 1st-century people by teaching and healing, with preaching and power. We can do the same in the power of the Spirit. Jesus proclaims a message of liberating truth and holistic healing. He does so by preaching the gospel of the kingdom of God. This gospel not only announces the Savior who forgives idolatrous pursuits of self but the King who reorders our distorted sense of being.

Jesus essentially says, *If you want your identity restored, you have to throw off your many masks or discard the idea of the modern, autonomous self, and embrace the one, true*

King. You've proven that self-rule is self-sabotage. Only I am fit to rule, and when I rule, I will straighten you out; your humanity will be restored. King Jesus overthrows the domineering powers that oppress humanity in order to make way for new eternal identities: beloved son, cherished daughter, justified sinner, saint, disciple, and redeemed new creation.

We must turn our backs on the old unfulfilling selves and give in to Christ to receive a renewed self. As Paul writes, "Do not lie to one another, seeing that you have put off the old self with its practices and have put on the new self, which is being renewed in knowledge after the image of its creator" (Colossians 3:9-10). Out of boundless compassion, Jesus essentially says, *Follow me. Live in my ways, believe my gospel, and it will change you forever. Unlike your other identities, this one will hold up. I will never change my opinion of you. You will always be mine—loved, adored, cherished, accepted—but you must give up your inferior identities and welcome me as Savior and Lord.*

We've observed that evangelism is both the heart of mission and the heart of Jesus. Far from being oppressive, sharing the good news with a harassed and helpless world is an act of compassion. When someone hears the gospel, repents of their sin, and believes in Jesus, they are rescued from fleeting and flawed identities that cannot satisfy. Instead, they are placed into Christ, who confers upon them undying love, perfect acceptance, and an eternal identity that does not change or disappoint.

With this in view, how should we go about sharing the gospel with others in a culture of resistance?

ACTION STEPS

- Write down three reasons why evangelism is plausible despite its unpopularity. Ask God to help you see people as he sees them.

- Take a moment to consider what it is like to be evangelized by a Christian. How might this alter the way you share your faith?

- Think of a non-Christian acquaintance. What identities or masks do they look to for significance? How could you share the gospel in a way that explains how Jesus offers them an identity that is better?

4. BIBLICAL EVANGELISM

"Read the Gospels to see how Jesus made the truth known. Every conversation Jesus had was different, for Jesus treated the people he met as individuals."
Jerram Barrs

While the word evangelism can stir up feelings of anxiety and fear, consider what it meant for *you* to hear the good news for the first time. Where were you when you internalized the notion that Christ suffered in your place to set you free from guilt, sin, and death, and rose to grant you forgiveness, righteousness, and new life as his beloved child? What did it feel like to respond to God's gracious offer of salvation in Jesus?

Did the gospel intrigue you? Perhaps you felt a sting of conviction, followed by a sense of freedom? Was it a humbling mixed with exhilaration? No wonder it's called the good news! That's what we get to share with others. Evangelism is getting the good news about Jesus into the bad and broken places of people's lives, and I'd like to help you do it in a way that isn't canned, forced, or manipulative but personal, Spirit-led, and thoughtful.

EVANGELISTIC TECHNIQUE

Many Christians have been trained in evangelistic techniques: for example, walk people through a gospel tract, draw a bridge diagram, sketch three circles, or memorize a script as you would in a sales job and rehearse it to the lost. While God has saved sinners through these techniques, there aren't examples of this kind of evangelism in the Bible. Of course, just because something isn't in the Bible, it doesn't mean it isn't biblically shaped or warranted. Just because there are no megachurches in the Bible, it doesn't mean a great number of people can't form a biblical church. However, some Christian practices can be so shaped by culture, not Scripture, that we miss significant truths.

Commenting on Western approaches to evangelism, British apologist Os Guinness notes that our preoccupation with technique "misses the independence of the biblical way of thinking and the brilliance and depth of the way of Jesus."[17] What kind of evangelism does Scripture commend to us? What brilliance and depth of Jesus might we be missing?

---

[17] Os Guinness, *Fool's Talk: Recovering the Art of Christian Persuasion* (IVP, 2015), p. 36.

Even a cursory glance through the Gospels reveals that Jesus never shared the gospel the same way twice. Instead, he approached each person as unique. He took into account their vocation, ethnicity, gender, religion, and location. With lawyers, he used legal reasoning; with rural people, he used agrarian metaphors (seed, harvest, weeds); with the wealthy, he spoke in financial terms (riches and poverty); with those seeking water, he promised to quench their spiritual thirst.

Similarly, the tract *Four Spiritual Laws*, for example, worked well with highly literate, rational modern people. In the late modern age, where people are more image focused and doubtful of the information they consume, evangelistic approaches like *Four Spiritual Laws* don't resonate in the same way. Since Jesus' evangelism was shaped by his hearers' culture, his evangelistic approach was not one size fits all.

THE EVANGELISM OF JESUS

Let's examine what we can learn from the evangelism of Jesus by considering his interaction with a rich, young ruler (Luke 18:18-25).[18]

A young, wealthy man comes to Jesus and inquires, "Good Teacher, what must I do to inherit eternal life?" (v 18). Can you imagine an easier evangelistic opportunity? This is a softball question, and Jesus misses it completely. He

---

18 To learn more about Jesus' evangelism, see Jerram Barrs, *Learning Evangelism from Jesus* (Crossway, 2009).

doesn't even answer it! Instead, Jesus responds by asking a counterquestion: "Why do you call me good? No one is good except God alone" (v 19). Why didn't Jesus simply tell the man to repent of his sins and believe to receive eternal life? It's because Jesus knew that evangelism is more than just conveying gospel information.

ASK QUESTIONS

Notice first that Jesus asks questions. He isn't preparing to rattle off a presentation. All too often we are waiting to give answers—to deliver the doctrine, win the argument, check the box. But Jesus responds with a question. Why? Because Jesus isn't seeking converts; he's engaging hearts. All too often our evangelism reduces people to projects. How many came to Christ this week? Did they pray the prayer? How many have you baptized this year? This approach is information driven. It doesn't take people's objections, idols, or concerns into account. But Jesus listens closely to those he evangelizes. How might your evangelism change if your aim was to understand people?

PAY ATTENTION TO WORDS

Next Jesus inquires, "Why do you call me good? No one is good except God alone" (v 19). Notice Jesus pays close attention to this man. He dignifies his vocabulary choice by asking him about the words he uses. "Good Teacher" would fly by a lot of us as we fixate on trying to get the cross into the conversation. We often angle to get a word in, but Jesus aims to draw him out.

Why does Jesus ask the religious ruler about goodness? New Testament commentators suggest several options:

1. Jesus is denying his own goodness, which doesn't comport with the rest of the gospel.

2. Jesus is redirecting him to Yahweh's goodness, making no commentary on himself.

3. Jesus of Nazareth is identifying himself with Yahweh's goodness, a radical claim to a Jewish ruler.

Jesus proceeds to discuss the law with the man—an area close to any synagogue ruler's heart.

FOCUS ON THE HEART

After the ruler insists that he has kept the law, Jesus responds to him by saying, "One thing you still lack. Sell all that you have and distribute to the poor, and you will have treasure in heaven; and come, follow me" (v 22). Instead of telling him to generically repent and believe, Jesus tells him to sell literally as much as he has and to give it to the poor. Why would Jesus, when asked how to inherit eternal life, tell someone to do good works? Aren't we saved by grace through faith alone?

Jesus is listening to the heart. His questions expose a works impulse in the man, for he asked Jesus, "What must I *do?*" His deepest desire is to *do something* for eternal life. The rich do-gooder is likely preoccupied with keeping the law, not clinging to Christ. He wants to achieve, not receive, salvation. In response, Jesus hits him where it hurts the most. We're told, "But when he heard these things, he became very sad, for he was extremely rich" (v 23).

The wealthy man's sadness reveals his idol. His riches occupy a God-sized place in his heart, and he is unwilling to part with them. If Jesus had simply told him to repent and believe, the ruler's functional god would have remained wealth. He could have said, "I believe," while trusting in himself. This would make him a Christian in name only, with a veneer of faith over an idolizing heart. But Jesus loves him enough to challenge him at the soul level. In order to gain eternal life, we have to surrender claims on our own life. Jesus is both the Redeemer *and* King.

USE A GOSPEL METAPHOR

First, Jesus dignifies the man, but then he devastates him by challenging the chief idol of his heart. We do a similar thing, but in a generic way, when we tell people they are sinful before a holy God. Most people would be flattered to be called good. So why does Jesus turn this compliment into such a penetrating question? Not to make the man miserable but to give him incomparable wealth: "You will have treasure in heaven; and come, follow me" (v 22).

Jesus communicates the gospel by using language that resonates with the rich man's longings—treasure. That treasure is a gospel metaphor—an image that compelled by God's grace to speak life and hope into the lives of others.

What matters most to a person with gracious speech? Winning the argument? Tying up everything in a bow? Forcing a person to pray a salvation prayer? No, the person with seasoned speech embraces the other person as they are. They engage in a variety of topics, recognizing the complexity of the person in front of them. Moving in and out of various topics with people, over time, allows us to get to know them. A seasoned relationship emerges in which we can discern how to speak words of gospel hope into their lives.

Answer Each Person
What does it look like to "answer each person"? When the apologist Francis Schaeffer was asked how he would spend an hour with someone who wasn't a Christian, he replied by saying he would listen for 55 minutes, and only in the last five minutes would he have something to say. Today, we often flip this; we want to talk for 55 minutes and then call for a response. Paul exhorts us to speak with others so that we are able to "answer each person." This implies that we are meaningfully engaged and able to offer personal counsel.

A wise, gracious evangelist matches personal need with specific gospel metaphors. There are scores of gospel metaphors in the Bible and scores of personal needs. In the next chapter, we will look at five key gospel metaphors and how to use them to walk with wisdom toward outsiders while using gracious speech and answering each person.

ACTION STEPS

- Take a moment to consider how Jesus' approach to evangelism differs from yours. What are a couple things you can refine or change in your evangelism?

- Think of a non-Christian acquaintance. Next time you talk to them, try to practice the things we see Jesus doing: ask questions, pay attention to words, listen to the heart.

- What gospel metaphor would best meet the deep longings of your non-Christian friend? Share that with them next time you can work it into a conversation.

5. GOSPEL METAPHORS

"If we are to fulfill our calling as a missional church in the 21st-century, we must reenact the task of singing the gospel in new keys that we see modeled in the writings and stories of the New Testament."
Dean Flemming

How can we follow Jesus' and Paul's examples of "answering each person" with wisdom and grace? What might it look like to become more fluent in speaking the gospel into peoples' lives? Let's consider five key gospel metaphors and how we can use them in evangelism.[20]

FIVE GOSPEL METAPHORS
Gospel metaphors stretch across the breadth of the Bible and communicate God's saving grace. The Old

---

[20] I have adapted this chapter from a fuller treatment of gospel metaphors in Jonathan K. Dodson, *The Unbelievable Gospel: Say Something Worth Believing* (Zondervan, 2014), p. 123-189.

Testament contains many redemptive metaphors, including inheritance, exodus, the multilayered metaphor of atonement, divine blessing, a new heart, and the new covenant. These various redemptive themes coalesce in the New Testament epistles into five central gospel metaphors: justification, redemption, adoption, new creation, and union with Christ. They are not metaphors in the sense that they stand for something else or that they are symbolic of some deeper reality. Rather, each gospel metaphor represents a very real grace. Together, they form facets of the "gospel of grace" diamond.[21]

Justification
This is a *legal* metaphor that resolves the dilemma of how the righteous God can relate to unrighteous people and still remain righteous. The solution to this dilemma is found in the person and work of Jesus Christ: "Yet we know that a person is not justified by works of the law but through faith in Jesus Christ" (Galatians 2:16).

The good news of justification is that while our works are sorely inadequate, Christ and his work are infinitely adequate to make us right before God. When we put our faith in Jesus, we are declared righteous based on his spotless righteousness. This makes us eternally

---

[21] While much more could be said about each metaphor, our focus here is to draw on a single aspect of each gospel facet for the sake of evangelism. For example, redemption contains a subset of gospel metaphors including: rescue, atonement, reconciliation, propitiation, expiation, and *Christus victor*.

accepted by God. Justification grants us perfect acceptance by the eternally righteous and loving God.

Justification makes the unacceptable eternally accepted by God.

Redemption
This is an *atonement* metaphor that deals with our guilt before our holy God. As sinners conceived in iniquity and guilty of sinful rebellion against God, we must pay the penalty for our sins, for "the wages of sin is death" (Romans 6:23). The price for crimes against the infinite God is an infinite punishment of eternal death.

But redemption means there is a grace-based alternative—a way to be pardoned that upholds God's holiness and forgives our sinfulness. In Jesus, a God-sized person takes our place by dying our death and absorbing our punishment: "In him we have redemption through his blood, the forgiveness of our trespasses, according to the riches of his grace" (Ephesians 1:7). Our overwhelming sin debt is paid off through Jesus' atoning work on the cross.

Redemption makes the guilty forever forgiven.

Adoption
This *familial* metaphor deals with our estrangement from God. In the gospel of adoption, our status is altered from orphans to children. Although we are born into this world as "children of wrath" (2:3), through the Father's electing love, we are relocated into his family as "children

of God" (1 John 3:1). This, too, happens through faith in Jesus: "In Christ Jesus you are all sons of God, through faith" (Galatians 3:26). Adoption is not a cold spiritual transaction but an affectionate choice: "In love he predestined us for adoption to himself as sons through Jesus Christ, according to the purpose of his will" (Ephesians 1:4-5). Because of God's adoptive love in Christ, we receive his enduring approval and enjoy fellowship with him.

Adoption gives enduring approval to those who don't belong.

New Creation
This is a *life-and-death* metaphor that changes our status and nature. In the gospel of new creation, what was dead is given new life. Although we are "dead in our trespasses," God makes us "alive together with Christ" (Ephesians 2:5). Jesus' triumph over death, his very resurrection life, is given to us. This new life is the eternal life imparted by the Holy Spirit. It is sometimes referred to as "regeneration" (Titus 3:5), which is a shedding of the old life and the birth of a new life within God's larger cosmic work of new creation.

New creation makes the dead eternally alive.

Union with Christ
This is a *mystical* metaphor that unites us intimately with Jesus. It is the integrating truth through which all

other gospel metaphors become true for us. If we are not united with Christ, we cannot enjoy any of his gospel benefits. But when we are united with Christ, we gain the world (1 Corinthians 3:22).

Union with Christ solves the bedrock problem of being divided from God. Apart from him, we cannot enjoy his grace, truth, and presence. But united with him, the whole train of gospel graces is intimately and eternally ours. Faith "in Christ" is the spiritual key that unlocks the storehouse of gospel riches, of which intimate, mystical union with Jesus is most precious.

Union with Christ brings those at enmity into intimacy with God.

In his abounding mercy and grace, God saves sinners through the redemptive interplay of these five gospel metaphors. The rejected are accepted; the guilty are forgiven; the orphan is adopted; the dead are brought to life; and the divided are united with Christ. It is truly glorious, but how do we bring this gospel glory into people's lives?

SHARING GOSPEL METAPHORS
You may have noticed the connection between human longing and gospel metaphors. As we listen to people's stories, we have the privilege of discerning which particular gospel metaphor connects with their innermost longing. By sharing the gospel through various biblical metaphors, we can bring the good news

into the bad and broken news of people's lives. Let's consider how to do this with a few examples.

Justification: Seeking Acceptance
Everyone has the good desire to be accepted—to know that we are welcome and won't be rejected. But for some, acceptance is the driving desire of their lives. They may seek acceptance from friends, colleagues, heroes, or even God. This may cause them to perform so that others will think well of them or to hide who they truly are, afraid that others will reject them. But the gospel of justification promises God's perfect acceptance through Jesus Christ, which floods us with tremendous relief and joy.

When I met James, he kept his hoodie up and spoke in short sentences. A dark cloud followed him everywhere. As we developed a friendship, he shared that he had been rejected as a child by his mother, who gave him up for adoption. This created a deep wound, which James tried to heal by finding worth in work, the army, travel, and friends, but none of it was enough. Eventually, he was reunited with his birth mother, but over time, she favored his older brother, which compounded his sense of rejection. His mom had her own issues and couldn't give James the love and acceptance he wanted.

As I listened to his story, I kept praying, asking God to give me good news for James. I immediately thought of the story of the prodigal son, so I told him how the father welcomed his prodigal son home not reluctantly but joyfully, forgiving him and welcoming him back into the family. I looked at James, who had tears streaming down his face, and said, "The Father is telling you it's time to come home, James. He loves you, forgives you, and accepts you perfectly in Christ." James fell into my chest and sobbed. He was overwhelmed by God's accepting love and put his faith in Jesus that day. James needed to know that the rejected could be accepted perfectly in Jesus. He needed to hear the gospel of justification.

Who do you know that is driven by the desire to be accepted? Take a moment to pray for them to be justified by faith in Christ. Next time you are with them, look for an opportunity to ask them questions, listen to their story, and speak the gospel of justification into their heart.

Redemption: Seeking the Uniqueness of Christ
The metaphor of redemption is powerful for those who are weighed down by guilt or paralyzed by religious options. One night I met a guy at a bar who challenged the uniqueness of Christianity by insisting that the devotees of Islam are just as sincere as Christians. He suggested that they are more sincere because they are willing to die for their faith. What makes Christianity unique?

I responded by sketching some of the major distinctions between Islam and Christianity. Then I made a simple observation about the uniqueness of Christ: in all major world religions, a religious code is devised to work our way to God. The problem, however, is that no one can keep the code. We are all guilty of moral and religious imperfection. But in Christianity, God works his way down to us. He keeps the code, upholds the moral law, and makes a way for us to be reconciled to God.

This is the unique thing about Christianity—grace. It is the fundamental difference between Christianity and other religions. The sincere self-sacrifice of Muslims, while noble, does not make us acceptable to a holy God. Rather, we need someone who is perfect to sacrifice for our failure to honor God and to present us acceptable to him. This is what Jesus did. No other religion offers this—where God is slain on behalf of his people, dies, rises from the dead, and then makes them acceptable, forgiven, and righteous. Explaining the uniqueness of Jesus and his atoning work clarified how Christianity is unique among the religious options Brian was considering.

I don't remember Brian's exact response that night. We continued to talk, and he continued to ask questions. There was some heavy head-nodding and a genuine openness to what I was saying. I lost touch with him, but then several years later, I discovered that Brian was helping lead worship in a local church, committed to the unique way of grace found in Jesus. You see, Christianity is unique not because Christians are better than other people but because Christ is better than all of us. Brian needed to hear how the gospel was unique, unlike any other religious perspective.

Who do you know that needs to hear about the uniqueness of God's redeeming grace? Begin praying for them now, asking the Spirit to open up an opportunity to share the gospel of redemption with them.

Adoption: Seeking Approval
The metaphor of adoption can be really powerful for people who feel like they don't belong. An intellectual gay friend of mine was dying from cancer, so I visited him in hospice. I entered the ice-cold, sterile room and walked up to his hospital bed. He lay there laboring to breathe, and he had lost so much weight that he looked like a bag of bones. I wondered, what would I want someone to ask me on my death bed?

I asked him to tell me about some of his favorite memories. He told me about how he had snuck into the White House, slipped into the greenroom of the *Today* show and hung out with famous actors, and consistently found himself in VIP rooms at concerts. We laughed about it, and then I asked him how he got into all those places. He replied, "Easy. I just acted like I belong. It's my life philosophy. If you act like you belong, you can get into just about anywhere."

Then it hit me. Scott had been acting like he belongs his whole life. So, I paused and said to him, "Scott, you know that won't work with God. He knows we don't belong. He knows all our sins. But that's why he sent his Son: to act perfectly and sacrificially on our behalf so we can belong forever and fully to him." I told him that I want to enjoy God's perfect love with him forever in God's new creation. By then, Scott had run out of energy, but he closed his eyes and nodded in agreement, and I prayed for him.

It was not like Scott to nod in agreement to anything he disagreed with. I hope that was an agreement of faith. I don't know for sure. But I do know that the Spirit opened up an opportunity to make the gospel real to him, and that it was a privilege to be by his side. Scott died several days later.

Do you know anyone who feels like they don't belong? Perhaps that feeling is hidden, like it was with Scott. What questions can you ask to uncover their deep longings and share the gospel of adoption with them?

New Creation: Seeking Hope

The metaphor of new creation can be especially compelling for people who are longing for a new start in life. People whose lives have been littered with failure, scarred by abuse, humbled through suffering, darkened by depression, or ruined by addiction. They need the hope of becoming a new creation. The gospel of new creation tells them that their old life can be exiled and a new life in Christ can be received, filling the hopelessness with hope.

I met Ben at rehab. He was disheveled and depressed, his teeth rotted by methamphetamines. I sat down with him and said, "Ben, I know this isn't what you dreamed of when you were a kid. Tell me how you got here." Ben told me that it was hard for him to find friends as a kid. He felt like he just didn't fit in with others, but eventually he found a community who welcomed him. His new friends were accepting, but when they pressured him to do drugs and he refused, he was alienated by his new community.

This rejection drove him to cope by smoking weed, which wasn't strong enough to dull his pain, so he tried stronger drugs. He developed a drug addiction, which drove him from his family and kept him from holding down a job. His life fell apart. Then a friend found him passed out on a sidewalk and checked him into the rehab center we were at. As I listened to his story, I asked the Holy Spirit to give me words that would bring him life. What should I say to such a sad story? Then it dawned on me—here is a young man who has aged beyond his years, whose life is in ruins; surely he wants a new life.

I said, "Ben, in the Bible, God promises new life to those who hope in Jesus. Through his death on the cross for you, he can exile your old life and make you a new creation. How does that sound?" He said, "Good. But I don't really believe in God, and I don't have shoes or a Bible." I told him I would return the next day with shoes and a Bible. We began reading it together, and eventually he decided he wanted to turn his life over to Christ. When he stood up in front of our church to share his story, he told everyone that God had delivered him from addiction and made him a new creation. He needed to hear the gospel of new creation—the hope that his old life could be exiled and a new life could take its place in Christ Jesus.

Who do you know that is longing for hope? Can you think of anyone who thinks their life is beyond repair? Take a moment to pray for them and ask God to make them a new creation. The next time you are with them, begin asking them questions about their life and look for opportunities to bring the hope of new creation into their life.

Union with Christ: Longing for Glory
The gospel metaphor of union with Christ is appealing to those who long for intimacy and glory. When we clothe ourselves with Christ, we put on a righteous presence more radiant, glorious, and beautiful than any workout, outfit, or diet could create for us.

I once counseled a woman who shared that she couldn't keep from compulsively working out. She exercised seven days a week, which caused some health problems. When I asked her why she couldn't stop, she confided, "I want people to notice me. When my body is chiseled, people look at me." She longed for glory and intimacy but settled for superficial attraction.

I explained that when we're clothed with Christ, we don't have to wear ourselves out to get God to notice. When we are united with Jesus, we are clothed with his very glory, so that when God looks at us, he sees the beauty of his Son. Paul reminds us that we have "Christ in [us], the hope of glory" (Colossians 1:27).

Do you know anyone who wants to be noticed? Who longs to be seen? Perhaps you could share with them how God doesn't just see us; he delights in us. When we repent of living for human attention and put our faith in Jesus, we gain the glorious gaze of Christ. The gospel of union with Christ offers us a loveliness and intimacy we can't find anywhere else.

If we listen to people's stories closely enough and ask enough questions, with the help of the Spirit, we can discern their deepest longings and show them how they can be fulfilled in Christ. We can connect the good news to their bad news and urge them to turn away from sin to enjoy our matchless Savior.

ACTION STEPS

- Which gospel metaphor is most appealing to you right now and why?

- Think of a non-Christian friend. What deep human longing do you see sitting on top of their story? Which gospel metaphor meets your friend's longing? Take some time to write down how you would share this with them, and then look for an opportunity to do so.

- Meet with others in your church to discuss and pray into how you can share the gospel in this kind of personal, attentive way that attracts others to the hope of Jesus.

6. COMMUNITY EVANGELISM

"One of the important methods of spreading the gospel in antiquity was the home."
Michael Green

None of the stories in this book could have been recorded without my church. In most cases, each person who heard a gospel metaphor from me also heard the gospel and saw its power in community. God uses this collective witness to rescue people out of darkness and place them into the kingdom of his beloved Son (Colossians 1:13). The church is the means of God's evangelistic genius, not isolated people with the gift of evangelism.

CONVERSION IS A COMMUNITY PROJECT

In fact, people rarely come to faith from a single gospel witness. Most conversions are the result of a process that occurs over time, and they involve a variety of different gospel testimonies, conversations, and experiences. Professor of evangelism Richard V. Peace writes, "Research indicates that no more than 30 percent of all conversions are punctiliar in nature. Most conversions take place over time, often with many fits and starts as one moves toward Jesus and his way. For most people conversion is a process, not an event."[22]

Of course, we are saved in a single moment through the regenerative work of the Holy Spirit (Titus 3:5). However, our reception of the gospel is a process and often comes from many different people. Communal witness is like laying logs in a firepit until the Spirit sparks the flame of faith.

If conversion is typically a process and not an event, it would be a disservice not to share some of the community's contributions from each story. Omitting them would not only dishonor the role others have played but also leave you with the unfortunate and inaccurate impression that successful evangelism really does hang on your individual witness. So, I'd like to circle back to some of these stories to bring out the roles played by others to demonstrate the importance of the local church in evangelism.

Ben's Small Group

In chapter 5, we met Ben, whose broken life of drug addiction was healed by the gospel hope of new creation.

---

22 Richard V. Peace, "Conflicting Understandings of Christian Conversion: A Missiological Challenge," *Overseas Mission Study Center Journal* 28 (2004) p. 8-14.

Ben's introduction to Jesus, however, was the result of a loving, witnessing gospel community. I met Ben in rehab, but how did he get there? His friend picked him up when he was strung out and got him to rehab. She accompanied me and introduced me to Ben when I visited him. After Ben got out of rehab, someone else in our church discipled him for a season, helping him get on his feet. But perhaps his most formative experience was becoming part of a small group—a Jesus-centered community that loved him through thick and thin.

His small group wasn't inwardly focused. They eagerly engaged with non-Christians and seekers, and it was with these people that Ben discovered true, Christ-centered community. They discussed and applied Sunday sermons, shared meals (Ben often made cupcakes), laughed, celebrated, and served the marginalized. Ben's experience with a witnessing community was instrumental in coming to faith in Jesus.

He heard the gospel explained and applied by this community, as they shared their own sin struggles and found hope in the forgiving, life-renewing Savior. Several of the relationships he developed in the small group were especially close. This smaller group of people helped him explore his doubts, encouraged his faith, and discipled him into a real understanding of the gospel.

This experience in a small group also taught Ben that he was saved into a community, not into a private relationship with Jesus. He learned that Jesus redeems us into his church. Many people played a role in guiding Ben to Christ.

People around James
Remember James, the man who was desperate for acceptance? I wouldn't have even met him if it wasn't for my wife. She encouraged me to attend the retreat where I met him. To be honest, I didn't want to go. At one point, I asked my wife to come pick me up. But then I met James, and I knew I needed to see the weekend through in order to love him and point him to Christ. I had no idea that James would actually repent of his sins and put his faith in Jesus that weekend.

But there were many people who connected with James that weekend. One lady spoke some powerful words to him about his family. A small group of people attentively listened to him as he shared his life story. Then there were the people who hosted and planned the retreat. After that weekend, I met James's grandparents, and they shared with me that they had been praying for him to come to faith in Jesus for *years*. It took a community to reach James with the gospel. Some prayed, some listened, some served, and some spoke the good news into his life. As a result, James met Jesus.

THE JESUS COMMUNITY
In chapter 2, we talked about being a missionary presence. This presence is both individual and corporate. God casts his saving light through our individual and our

collective witness. This was also true of Jesus' ministry. When he started his public ministry, he didn't go it alone. He selected twelve men and depended on a cohort of women, and together they changed the world.

After Jesus was crucified, the community that had formed around him remained together. They met in a room where they comforted one another, fellowshiped, and prayed. All the followers of Jesus were connected to one another because they were profoundly connected in Christ. They learned to share just about everything: meals, prayers, evangelism, sermons, lessons with the Master, feeding the poor, communion, persecution, the promises of God, and the hope of Christ's return. Jesus didn't just "make disciples"; he made a new family: "And looking about at those who sat around him, he said, 'Here are my mother and my brothers!'" (Mark 3:34). Jesus drew people to himself and to one another. Our life together is meant to be a countercultural witness to the power and hope of the gospel.

From the Bible's perspective, community isn't optional. New Testament scholar Joseph Hellerman notes, "We do not find an unchurched Christian in the New Testament ... A person was not saved for the sole purpose of enjoying a personal relationship with God ... A person is saved to community."[23]

---

23 Joseph H. Hellerman, *When the Church Was a Family: Recapturing Jesus' Vision for Authentic Christian Community* (Broadman & Holman, 2011), p. 123–24.

If you are not meaningfully connected to other disciples, you haven't embraced the implications of your union with Christ. You haven't fully realized the meaning of your adoption into a new family. You have an important role to play in the church bearing witness to the world. Your spiritual gifts, personality, experiences, and relationship with Jesus are a vital part of the community's witness to Christ.

I cannot connect to every person on my own. I have people around me who have their own particular talents and passions, and I see how the Lord has gifted them to reach all kinds of people. Haydn is a good friend, a sincere follower of Jesus, and an avid cyclist. If I got on a road bike, I would probably fall off, so when I meet people who are into cycling, I often connect them to Haydn. His hobby connects him to non-Christians in a way that I just can't. I know Haydn will look for opportunities to point people to the Lord.

Luke is brilliant. He has a master's degree from Oxford University in sociology, he has launched multiple start-ups, and he thinks deeply about everything. So, when I meet intellectuals or entrepreneurs who don't know Jesus, I often introduce them to Luke. And he becomes a life-giving gospel witness to them.

Loma is head of a department at a multinational corporation that serves Fortune 500 companies. She is widely respected in her company and very open about her faith. People come to her often with spiritual questions, and when her small group gathers, she updates us on those questions, asks for wisdom, and enlists our prayer for her colleagues.

Eileen is a single artist who loves to connect with other people. Every other week she brings a new person to church. How does she do it? She is transparent with others about how God inspires her art and how much she loves her church. People feel impelled to come.

THE HOSPITABLE COMMUNITY

In his landmark book, *Evangelism in the Early Church,* scholar Michael Green observes, "One of the important methods of spreading the gospel in antiquity was the home."[24] Homes were the base for gospel ministry. Lydia in Philippi opened her doors, Jason used his home in Thessalonica, Titius Justus in Corinth, and Philip in Caesarea (Acts 16:15; 17:7; 18:7; 21:8). The home is still a key context for evangelism, which means hospitality is an important part of the church's witness. Biblical hospitality involves more than having a spotless home for your friends and neighbors. It's having an open door: a place of warm welcome to the rich and the poor, the lost and the saved, the easy and the demanding, friends and strangers.

My wife, Robie, exudes hospitality. We have people in our home from church, the neighborhood, and work

---

[24] Michael Green, *Evangelism in the Early Church* (Eerdmans, 2004), p. 318.

just about every week. Robie loves to host parties on a monthly basis. She goes out of her way to engage with non-Christians, make conversation with newcomers, and generate a joyful atmosphere for all. She creates a context where Christian and non-Christian alike can share a good time, lots of Costco food, gospel conversations, and laughter! We've been in a new neighborhood for about six months and have already had 50 neighbors over. Thanks to the welcoming, loving home my wife has created (and our great kids) we get to know all kinds of people.

I've gotten to know Buddhists, secularists, agnostics, and atheists all through her hospitality. Well, it's a shared endeavor, but honestly, I would never throw these parties if I wasn't married to her! We intentionally mix up Christians and non-Christians, and our neighbors regularly comment on how much they enjoy our church friends. Many of these social events have played a role in the evangelistic stories I have shared.

I tell these stories to show that evangelism is a community project. The church is God's missionary genius for the world. Your gifts, personality, hobbies, history, and faith are an important part of giving collective witness to the saving grace of Jesus Christ. I hope you're inspired to lean into your church, deepen relationships in community, and invite non-Christians into the Jesus community. After all, a chorus of gospel voices is much stronger than a lone witness in the wind.

ACTION STEPS

- What can you do to cultivate community evangelism within your relationships? Is there a Christian brother or sister you could introduce to a non-believing friend who might be able to connect with them naturally?

- Think of a person with the gift of hospitality. Send them a message to encourage them in their important role in evangelism.

- When you next meet with your small group or church friends, pray together for the work of the Holy Spirit in the lives of specific people you know. Keep accountable to each other in asking how those friends are doing.

7. SHAMELESS PRAYER

The knowledge, then, that God is sovereign in grace, and that we are impotent to win souls, should make us pray and keep us praying."
J.I. Packer

Screen writer and director Miranda July was on her way to return a book to the library when suddenly the man in front of her collapsed onto her, unresponsive.[25] She shouted for help until a security guard showed up and called emergency medical services. As she waited, the collapsed man's face began to turn gray-blue; a nearby friend started to lose it, whimpering, "What do we do? What do we do?" So she said, "Let's pray."

---

25 Miranda July, "Doing Nothing Isn't Enough" *The New Yorker*, June 2020.

Miranda had no idea how to pray, so she did what she'd seen in the movies: laid her hands on the man's shoulders, bowed her head, and begged with all her heart for the man to live. When is the last time you begged God for someone to truly live? We often don't pray for others until we're forced to, until circumstances demand it, until death is at our door. But what if we prayed for the spiritually dead with desperation now?

BEG LIKE A FRIEND

After instructing his disciples in devotional prayer (Luke 11:1-4), Jesus taught them about intercessory prayer. I like how a friend of mine describes intercessory prayer: as "talking to God on behalf of others." There are no praying elites in the kingdom of God. Anyone can talk to God on behalf of others. But how should we do it?

Jesus tells the story of a man who receives a traveler at midnight after a long journey. The traveler has had no drive-thru to grab a bite on the way, so he arrives famished. With nothing to offer his guest, the host goes next door and asks his friend for three loaves of bread. What's the point of the story? We can learn two things.

First, notice Jesus' opening question: "Which of you who has a friend will go to him?" (v 5). Who wouldn't go to a friend at midnight in a real pinch? One evening our infant daughter started struggling to breathe. It got worse and worse; we needed to rush her to the ER. But our other toddler was asleep. Even though it was late, I called my friend and asked, "How soon can you get here?" When things are urgent, we turn to our friends, no matter how inconvenient it is. Do you know people in urgent need? People who need healing, strength, faith, grace, salvation? Pray without hesitation. Don't hesitate to turn to your greatest friend, Jesus Christ, and ask him for help. He's never inconvenienced. We aren't interrupting. He's eager to hear our prayers and meet our needs.

Second, notice that the friend in the story objects. Jesus says, "I tell you, though he will not get up and give him anything because he is his friend, yet because of his impudence he will rise and give him whatever he needs" (v 8). Another thing we learn from the story is that though his friend can't be roused by friendship, he will be roused by impudence. The Greek word for "impudence" means to be shameless or persistent. Moreover, the man uses an imperative: "Lend me three loaves!" Thus, Jesus is teaching us to pray confidently and persistently, to intercede with fire in the belly. Jesus is not like the friend who can't be roused; he is always ready to respond to our need. So how much more should we ask him to help us and not give up asking!

After the murder of George Floyd, we had an impromptu prayer vigil at my church. During that prayer time, people cried out for justice for black Americans, who endure racism in our country: profiling, police brutality, overcriminalization, disproportionate incarceration rates, and murder. Don't give up. If you're not praying, start interceding. In an article entitled, "Prayer is

Activism," Eugene Park reminds us, "When we pray in times of injustice, we are protesting to the highest authority in the universe, the perfect arbiter of all justice."[26] We should pray desperately out of great need for justice and for eternal salvation.

People are in desperate need of redemption. The gospel compels us to pray not only for people's physical needs but for their eternal needs. Jesus said, "Whoever believes in the Son has eternal life; whoever does not obey the Son shall not see life, but the wrath of God remains on him" (John 3:36). Could there be anything more urgent? Eternal life and death are on the line. Pray that your family, friends, and neighbors will not suffer the eternal wrath of God but receive eternal life.

To be honest, this kind of praying rises and falls in my life. There are seasons when I walk around my neighborhood and beg God for the salvation of my neighbors and days I flat out forget. There are times when I'm passionate to pray for justice and times when I'm not. Jesus' story reminds us to pray unhesitatingly and shamelessly—to beg like a friend at the midnight hour.

PRAY LIKE AN UNEQUAL

Will God really answer our prayers? Jesus says, "For everyone who asks receives, and the one who seeks finds, and to the one who knocks it will be opened" (Luke 11:10).

---

[26] Eugene Park, "Prayer Is Activism," The Gospel Coalition, June 11, 2020.

The door will be opened. God answers every single prayer. But not always in the way we want. Sometimes it feels as if the door to our prayers is locked shut.

Jesus also teaches us to pray, "Hallowed be your name. Your kingdom come, your will be done" (Matthew 6:9-10). Prayer is not a way to leverage God to do our bidding. If that were so, we would be the god. Instead, Jesus teaches us to pray in *reverent submission*. We ask for help and to hallow his name.

You may feel the tension between shameless petition and reverent submission. Which is it? Are we to beg God or trust God? The answer is both! You beg for help from those you trust. If you're desperate enough, you beg for help from those you don't know well enough to trust, as the man did in Jesus' parable in Luke 11. But our heavenly Father is fully trustworthy so we will never be in that position. We can always ask and always trust that he will answer in the way that is best for our good.

In my early twenties, weighed down by shame, I asked God to take my life. I'm grateful he didn't. I've also asked for unwise things: for example, wishing to marry a girlfriend who didn't become my wife. I'm thrilled God didn't answer that prayer or else I wouldn't be married to Robie! We pray in reverent submission to God's will because God is wiser and kinder than we could ever be.

If we don't have confidence that God has given us prayer as a way to communicate with him, we probably won't even pray. That puts us out of touch with God. But if we know that we have the chance to speak with the most powerful, most loving, most wise being in the universe, we'd be fools not to.

To refuse to intercede in prayer is to miss out on God's power. If we don't pray, we won't get to see him work in response to our prayers in powerful ways. I think of the people I've prayed for who have been baptized or our friends who couldn't conceive but then became pregnant and had twins. But we pray as unequals. Jesus instructs us to pray not *my* will be done but *thy* will be done. To him, not us, belongs the hallowing and glory.

As we voice our needs and the needs of others, it's important to recognize that God has what scholar Gordon T. Smith calls a "privileged voice."[27] The final objective of prayer is not in our request but in allowing God to speak—for him to have the final word. So while prayer is two-way communication, it is not communication between peers but unequals. We speak to an omniscient and omnipotent king. And like a king, God often seeks to conquer and occupy rebellious territory in our hearts. He may expose false beliefs, convict us of sin, or redirect our decisions. When we pray in reverent submission, we avoid foolish

---

27 Gordon T. Smith, *The Voice of Jesus* (IVP, 2015), p. 163.

prayers and get aligned with God himself. We pray as an unequal.

TRUST LIKE A CHILD

My children ask for outlandish things. Can we have a house with a pool? Can we stay in a hotel (during Covid)? And sometimes they get them! We stayed at an Airbnb with a pool during Covid. Jesus says, "What father among you, if his son asks for a fish, will instead of a fish give him a serpent; or if he asks for an egg, will give him a scorpion?" (Luke 11:11-12). What is his point? *Trust me*, like a child trusts his father.

Generally speaking, parents are trustworthy; we want to give our children good things, not bad things. So, if a child asks for something good—an edible fish or egg, we don't give them something that bites or stings in return. But we might not give a good gift right away. When our kids were young, I denied their requests (pleadings) for an iPhone for years. Why? Because I'm a tyrant? No, because I knew they weren't ready to access the world and for the world to access them. How much more does our heavenly Father know when we are ready for his good gifts? So ask, but ask like a child—with complete trust, knowing some good things won't be given immediately or that God has something for us that he knows is better than what we are seeking.

This is also true in seeking the peace of our towns and cities. God doesn't immediately grant justice for the oppressed and salvation for those stranded in sin. Like a wise parent, he has his reasons. It's not always prudent for us to know why. In fact, some of his reasons are so supremely complex in working out his sovereign plan that we probably couldn't handle the explanation. But we can trust him, like a child—like an unequal. He's given us every reason to do so. The cross reminds us that God sent Christ to take the greatest punishment to give us the greatest gift—the Spirit!

Jesus reminds us, "If you then, who are evil, know how to give good gifts to your children, how much more will the heavenly Father give the Holy Spirit to those who ask him!" (v 13). Why is the Spirit the greatest gift? First, the Spirit is God with us; we don't have to climb a mountain or go to a temple to hear his voice. We have the mobile very presence of God at all times.

Second, the Spirit prays with us, nudging us to enjoy the Father's love, to intercede for a friend, to plead for justice, and to ask for salvation (Romans 8:26-27). When we receive the Spirit, we get to commune with him and participate in God's sovereign and saving plan for the world. Third, the Spirit gives us more excellent gifts: love, joy, peace, patience, kindness, goodness, faithfulness, gentleness, and self-control (Galatians 5:22-23). Doesn't the world need those gifts right now?

Death is at the doorstep of everyone around us. People face a Christless eternity. Many are desperate to hear that God in Christ lifts their burdens—that he is eager to bless them with eternal joy and peace. Others can't imagine the hope of becoming a new person, an adopted and beloved child, a forgiven sinner, or an intimately known and accepted person. But we have this good news, so let's share it!

We also know the most loving, wise, and powerful being in the universe, who invites our requests. So let's pray! Beg like a friend, confidently; pray like an unequal, reverently; and inquire like a child, trustingly. God is eager to hear our requests. He possesses perfect wisdom, knowing just how to answer them, and the cross of Christ reminds us that he, of all people, can be trusted with our deepest concerns.

ACTION STEPS

- How might "reverent submission" and "trusting like a child" influence some of your current prayers for yourself and for those who don't know Jesus? Share your thoughts with God.

- To increase persistent prayer in your life, think of an injustice in the world and a non-Christian whom you can pray for on Mondays. Mondays are for mission!

- How does your church come together in prayer for the lost? You could do a regular prayer walk in the vicinity of the church, asking God to draw those living in the local area to himself and for the softening of their hearts to the gospel message.

CONCLUSION

The mission of God is both grand and microscopic; it is as big as the cosmos and as small as you and me. The Father, Son, and Holy Spirit have embarked on a renewal project that changes everything, and God has chosen to include us. The Lord does not have a Plan B for his mission. You are his Plan A. The church is God's true witness to the world. Consider this story of how the church witnessed to Mark:[28]

> *Atheist. That's a strong word, but it was one that partly defined me. I was arrogant and proud in counting myself out of the needy crowd. I could face the stark fact that we are just the result of billions of years of randomness and that the unfortunate answer to 'what is the meaning of life?' was simple: there is no meaning. We're here just by the happenstance of physics*

---

28 "Coming to Christ," a personal essay, August 25, 2018.

and chemistry that played out. I was okay with that, thinking I was smart enough to face these facts.

Mark goes on to describe hearing the gospel message in his childhood church, "but I'm not sure I ever really listened." From there he went to college, where he concluded that Christianity was just "another myth alongside the Greek ones." He got married, cheated on his wife, divorced, and became estranged from his children, but he didn't believe there were moral missteps, only unfortunate outcomes—he lived in a scientific world.

But then Mark met Amy. After marrying her, he discovered that "God used the person closest to me, working through my wife and friend, who I love with all my heart. God showed me his power through her." Amy also shared the gospel with Mark. He then visited several other churches and heard the good news there, but when he landed at City Life Church, he described entering into "a community in relationship with God that I have never before experienced." At City Life Mark heard the gospel and experienced love, forgiveness, and acceptance like never before.

On August 28, 2018, Mark was baptized before his witnessing church family. He emerged from the baptismal waters with his arms shooting straight up into the sky, a smile plastered across his face as he relished his newfound salvation. Looking back, he writes, "Jesus was my steady pursuer, waiting for the time when I would accept grace where it was totally undeserved."

There are many people like Mark who need to hear the good news. And notice that he heard the gospel many times, from various people, in different churches, over the course of decades. Don't write off anyone from the redeeming grace of God. Jesus loves to rescue atheists, adulterers, skeptics, and sinners. There are many more people who have not yet been touched by God's redeeming grace.

We, the church, have been entrusted with news that brings the beauty of redemption into the broken places of this world. We have friends and family that need to know the belonging, intimacy, acceptance, hope, and forgiveness that only Jesus Christ offers. Many unreached people groups around the world still need to hear the good news.

So, let's slow down and listen to people's stories, ask them questions, uncover their heart longings, and point them to saving grace in Christ. May we find ourselves talking more about Jesus because we too are taken with Jesus.

ACKNOWLEDGMENTS

I am grateful not only to have written but also lived this book alongside my former church, City Life. We truly lived together as a missionary community in the heart of Austin, Texas, where we witnessed the Spirit of God make men, women, and children new in Christ Jesus.

I am also grateful to Rob Berreth and Claude Atcho for their hearty approval of adaptation of material from my book, *Mission*, written for the Foundations series. You can find out more about this curriculum for church-based theological training at equipthesaints.org.

A special thank-you to Zondervan for granting permission to reproduce my work on gospel metaphors here and for their generous support of what became an award-winning book, *The Unbelievable Gospel*.

Finally, I conclude with a few lines from the poet Malcolm Guite, who writes:

I cannot think unless I have been thought,
Nor can I speak unless I have been spoken;
I cannot teach except as I am taught...[29]

Lord Christ, I thank you for thinking of me, speaking through me, and for all who have taught me. May this short book bring your blessing to all who read it.

---

[29] Malcolm Guite, *Sounding the Seasons: Seventy Sonnets for the Christian Year* (Canterbury Press Norwich, 2012), p. 7.

DISCUSSION GUIDE FOR SMALL GROUPS

1. TRUE WITNESS

1. What is beautiful to you about God?

2. *Read Hebrews 1:1-4.* What is beautiful and unique about Jesus in these verses?

3. What other Bible passages or stories fill you with excitement about who Jesus is and what he has done?

4. Think of a time when the actions of a Christian believer made the beauty of Jesus come alive for you. What did they do, and how did it make a difference to you? (See the author's example on page 16.)

5. How easy do you find it to talk about Jesus? How did this chapter make you feel about that?

6. What could you do this week to cultivate being more taken with Jesus?

2. FAITHFUL PRESENCE

1. *Read Jeremiah 29:4-7.* What should the Israelites' attitude be to the foreign city they are living in?

2. Assuming these instructions were followed, how might God's people have ended up blessing those around them?

3. Practically speaking, what could it look like for you to be an economic and social blessing in your community, and to help heal what is broken? (Take a look at the bullet points on pages 33-35 if you're stuck for ideas.) Consider what steps you might take this week, this month, and this year.

4. Why is it a challenge to live a holy life, yet engage with the secular world around us? Are there particular issues or situations where you feel this tension?

5. What did you think of the ideas for prayer on pages 36-37? Could you put anything like this into practice?

6. *Read Colossians 1:20* and spend some time praying for individuals you know who don't know Jesus yet. Ask God to bring "full-orbed shalom" into their lives, and pray for his help as you seek to communicate the message of Christ.

3. IMPLAUSIBLE EVANGELISM

1. How do you generally feel about evangelism? Do you ever feel that it's "implausible"? Did any of the reasons to avoid evangelism listed on pages 46-51 resonate with you?

2. Reread the section "Compassionate Evangelism." What did you find helpful about this description of Jesus' evangelism?

3. *Read Romans 1:18-25.* How does this help you make sense of what is going on spiritually in the hearts of unbelievers? Can you think of some real-life examples? (The section "Many Identities" may help with this.)

4. "The only way for the spiritually resistant to be liberated into the saving love of Jesus Christ is for someone to preach the gospel to them. Spiritual death and resistance can be overturned by a single, eternal, powerful word shared by an ordinary Christian." *Read 1 Peter 1:3-5 and 23-25* and consider what these verses say about being born again. How does this make you feel about sharing God's word with others?

5. In pages 54-56, Dodson writes about how Jesus transforms our identity. Could you write your own short summary of the gospel message in a way that might resonate with people struggling with identity issues?

6. In what other ways is the message of Jesus good news for those around us today?

4. BIBLICAL EVANGELISM

1. "Jesus knew that evangelism is more than just conveying gospel information." How would you sum up what evangelism is? How has reading this chapter influenced your answer?

2. *Read Luke 18:18-25.* Imagine you were having a conversation like this today. In what ways are Jesus' words different from what you might expect a modern evangelist to say?

3. Look back at the headings on pages 61-64. Why could each of these be a valuable part of our evangelism? How confident do you feel about putting each of these into practice?

4. Think about some non-Christians you know. What do you think is "the one thing each of them is unwilling to give up"? How could that help you speak to them about Jesus? (Look back at pages 64-66 if you need help with this.)

5. *Read Colossians 4:5-6.* Consider these verses slowly. What could it look like to put each piece of advice into practice? What help do you need from God? You might find it helpful to write out the phrases separately on large pieces of paper and then write your ideas around each one. (Look back at pages 67-69 if you need help for more ideas.)

6. "Paul is describing a person who is deeply interested in others ... [They are not] poised to condemn, nor are they afraid to speak; they are compelled by God's grace to speak life and hope into the lives of others." Pray for one another that, by his grace, God would turn you into this kind of person.

5. GOSPEL METAPHORS

1. Could you quickly summarize the "five central gospel metaphors"—justification, redemption, adoption, new creation, and union with Christ? What does each mean, in simple language?

2. Which of these resonates most with you personally? Can you explain why?

3. Imagine you're using one of the gospel metaphors to explain to a non-Christian what Jesus has done for you. How would you explain it to them, using ordinary words?

4. How confident do you feel about discerning what is driving the non-Christians you talk to, and which gospel metaphor might be most helpful for them? What could help you get better at this?

5. Choose one of the gospel metaphors and look at the Bible passages mentioned by Dodson in connection with it. What does each one tell you? How might you explain each verse to an unbelieving friend?

6. Spend some time praising God for all that he has done for us in Christ. Then turn your praises into prayers for the salvation of those you know and love.

6. COMMUNITY EVANGELISM

1. *Read 1 Corinthians 12.* What does it mean to be part of the body of Christ? Do you ever fall into the trap of thinking some people (maybe yourself, maybe others) are less valuable or important?

2. What would you say your gifts and strengths are? What are you less good at? What would it look like for the members of your group to support one another in each other's weaknesses? (Think about any area of life, not just evangelism.)

3. What could it look like for the members of your group to support one another in evangelism? For example, imagine you meet someone with whom you don't have much in common. What steps could you take to connect that person with someone who "speaks their language" a bit more? Or, imagine an unbeliever came to your small group. What would you do to make them welcome and help them learn about Jesus?

4. Why is it so valuable to connect unbelieving friends with different Christians you know?

5. Do you see your home as a place for evangelism? Why, or why not? What could you do to use your home for evangelism?

6. *Reread 1 Corinthians 12:12-14,* and pray for God's help and wisdom as you all seek to reach out as a body.

7. SHAMELESS PRAYER

1. "There are times when I ... beg God for the salvation of my neighbors and days I flat out forget." How would you describe your own willingness to pray for the salvation of others at the moment?

2. *Read Luke 11:1-13.* What does this passage teach us about our heavenly Father?

3. How should this impact the way we pray?

4. *Read John 3:36.* Who do you know who is facing the sobering reality in the second part of the verse? How often do you think about how desperate their need is?

5. God promises to give us the Holy Spirit when we ask him. *Read Romans 8:26-27.* How do these verses encourage you and spur you on in prayer?

6. Spend some time discussing your experiences with evangelism and those you would like to pray for. Then use the Lord's Prayer (Luke 11:2-4) to help you pray for yourselves and others.

LOVE YOUR CHURCH

gather — Tony Merida (Foreword by David Platt)
Loving your church as you celebrate Christ together

welcome — Jen Oshman (Foreword by Tim Challies)
Loving your church by making space for everyone

belong — Barnabas Piper (Foreword by Ray Ortlund)
Loving your church by reflecting Christ to one another

serve — Steve Robinson (Foreword by Brian Howard)
Loving your church with your heart, time, and gifts

send — Jim Essian (Foreword by Joby Martin)
Loving your church by praying, giving, or going

honor — Adam Ramsey (Foreword by Alistair Begg)
Loving your church by building one another up

care — Dwayne Bond (Foreword by Jonathan D. Holmes)
Loving your church by walking through life together

witness — Jonathan K. Dodson (Foreword by Ed Stetzer)
Loving your church by sharing the gospel

loveyourchurchseries.com

2015 Christianity Today Award: Best Book on Evangelism

Jonathan Dodson diagnoses the evangelistic paralysis of the modern church and offers a desperately needed solution. Filled with stories that reveal the long road of relational evangelism and guidance on how to communicate and listen to others well. A much-needed resource that will benefit both individuals and churches.

thegoodbook
COMPANY

BIBLICAL | RELEVANT | ACCESSIBLE

At The Good Book Company we are dedicated to helping Christians and local churches grow. We believe that God's growth process always starts with hearing clearly what he has said to us through his timeless and flawless word—the Bible.

Ever since we opened our doors in 1991, we have been striving to produce resources that are biblical, relevant, and accessible. By God's grace, we have grown to become an international publisher, encouraging ordinary Christians of every age and stage and every background and denomination to live for Christ day by day and equipping churches to grow in their knowledge of God, their love for one another, and the effectiveness of their outreach.

Call one of our friendly team for a discussion of your needs or visit one of our local websites for more information on the resources and services we provide.

Your friends at The Good Book Company

thegoodbook.com | thegoodbook.co.uk
thegoodbook.com.au | thegoodbook.co.nz